www.trafford.com

North America & international
toll-free: 1 888 232 4444 (USA & Canada)
phone: 250 383 6864 ♦ fax: 812 355 4082

Staged Affair

. . . a dramancedy . . .

Frank W. Bosworth

Other titles by this author:
Never Play Leapfrog with a Unicorn

In memory of
Linda Bosworth-Belanger

Between life's *dra*ma,
ro*manc*e & com*edy* lies the
dramancedy.

~Contents~

Prologue

Staged Affair

But for gender, and maybe age, we're not much different, you and I.

You. Yes, you.

Our dreams, our deepest desires may differ, but it's the little things, those little everyday things we have in common. For example, time. We all steal time. Sought after by each of us daily, we allocate, allow and, yes, steal away from the day-to-day grind for just a minute's peace of mind. We cherish those few, precious, personal minutes for ourselves, ourselves alone. We may escape to a good book, write out a long lost memory, balance the checkbook, contemplate our navel lint. There has to be a zillion personal satisfiers.

My favorite as more 'n more time slips by? I like to nap. Oh, and write, in that order.

On occasion, after all respected, well-intended, yes, even unsolicited advice has been entertained, that is, filtered and strained, we must steal time to sit back, ponder, toss around, weigh, and finally make an important decision. Yes, even a life-altering decision or two. You know, not any old run-of-the-mill decision, but a one-shot roll of the dice life reassessment, a 'realignment of priorities' decision.

The good ones, the vibrant ones, the decisions that leave us charged, piss'n vinegar enriched anew, seem to happen in a lifetime's first half. Decisions made in the second half, the half with more yesterdays, fewer tomorrows, well, they seem to be all about roughage, liver spots, AARP, and burial plots. I am making jest . . . sort of.

At this writing, if I live to the ripe old age of one hundred and six, then, yes, you could say I'm middle-aged. *'Hm, one hundred and six?'* No, that's a bit much. I do hope to see eighty and a day though. If I'm still kicking enough to see the sun rise on that extra day, if at dawns break I find I'm terminally anything—including old and alone—I'll bow out at my own hand. I have given thought to the setting. All this day will require are; the clothes on my back, a Colorado mountain ledge, a blazing sunset—blessed by Saints, kissed by Angels—and a fatty I've been hoarding for just this day. Oh, and Thee.

Set in a time of my life still rich in dreams, when tomorrows were so plentiful they easily outnumbered but a scant few yesterdays, this is a hope, a wish, a one-finger salute good-bye to the suburban shuffle hum story.

This is a true story.

A true tunnel vision story.

~~~

Center Stage ~ Biltmore Ballroom ~ Central Park & Broadway ~ New York City

'The Roar of the Greasepaint, the Smell of the Crowd,' I thought, grinning, as behind the closed curtain I made my way across the darkened stage. I counted the paces, eleven, and sat down on the pre-set old wicker rocker, stage front center. *'Well, so far, so good. I didn't trip.'*

Though mere seconds ticked by til my 'act' was announced, my name introduced, I felt I had aged a decade. *'How? How in the name of hell did I get here? Oh, now is a fine time to question a moment!'* No time to dally, to ponder. *'Breathe! Concentrate!'*

The heavy, red velvet curtain slowly rose. A bank of powder blue baby-spots came up, illuminating, framing the staged scene. Chosen background music came in, setting the atmosphere. In front of me, left and right of the center aisle, front to back, rolled a sea of eyes. I looked up to the gilt-edged balcony, to a wave of more eyes gazing down. The monster stared back, silent. For a millisecond (blank) I forgot the first word (choke).

My mind flew, racing through hundreds of memory files, of present thoughts, of future ideas, searching. Then, as I listened, as if in disembodied verbal cruise control, the first line, cloaked in a smooth, put-on, aged tumble, came out.

"Ah, yes, another year past . . ."

I heard a voice in my head, well, not one, but many voices of support, of encouragement, from way back when. *'This is it, boy. Stick it! It all comes down to this. You made these three minutes happen. Reach in, grab hold, rip their friggen hearts out!'*

"ah, but what a year it was."

'Listen. Do you hear it?' Despite the light background music, and over my voice, I could have heard the proverbial pin drop. *'Do you hear, twerp? Nothing. You got 'em, you got 'em right where you want 'em,'* My mind raced placing faces to voices from my 'family bush', as words, my words, committed to memory, poured out.

"Now, I look across the tables . . ."

'They have no idea what's coming, but you do, bunghole, you do. You wrote it, and they're listening.'

"see the same old faces . . ."

'Listen. Silence. They were not expecting you. They certainly were not expecting this.'

"hear the same old fables."

'They're all yours, boy. What was is no longer. Say hello to what is, knucklehead.'

~~~

In the scheme of things, it was a little dream.
In the scheme of dreams, it was everything.

~1~

Finding the Thread

**My kitchen,
four months earlier.**

~~~

"You might do what? Quit? You're joking! You're serious? What're
you, high? If not, you should be!" Rick finished rolling a gem,
laughed, and sparked up. "Here."

We had been friends for a couple of years. Like most of the people
I knew at the time, Rick lived in the city. I rented a cottage on the
beach. If you have ever experienced a New England Atlantic coastline
winter, you know 'living at the beach' is not as idyllic as it sounds,

but from September to June the rent's cheap, solitude priceless, the ocean at once inspiring and, in a wink, threatening with fury.

"No, see, you don't get it," I continued, stressing my point. "Your uncle's in the union, right? A boilermaker? And what do you want to do? What're you going to be? He's your in, your contact. He'll punch your card; you'll be set in the union too, right?"

"So? A contact's a contact. You took the exam, got in the Post Office."

"A part-time, flex, temp."

"So, you're not getting your forty hours yet. Still, that's not a nothing job. There'll be openings. People come and go." He paused, then guffawed, "and die!"

"Not exactly something you can hang your hat on while you're waiting," I semi-argued.

"You don't need an in somewhere, you're in, somewhere." His brow furrowed, amused/confused by his own words.

"Okay, take another toke." I chuckled, he laughed.

Rick was about twenty-two, roughly three years younger than me. A laid back, easy going type of guy, more a realist, not much of an optimist, an animated listener, someone I could bounce ideas off. He spoke little, smoked a lot. His opinions were never overstated, usually concise, to the point. His wants concerned today. Anything beyond 'now' was fate and fat chance.

"What's it matter how you got there? You're in; it's a good job. Don't blow it."

"But, that's it! A job! It's just a job!" I gazed out the perfectly placed picture window, lost in thought. 'Perfectly placed' because, while sitting at the kitchen table, you had a picture-perfect coastline view. I sat staring, seeing nothing. "There has to be more."

"More to what?" he questioned, fingers snapping to get my attention. "Earth to—"

"In the last month, I saw a carrier remove an eight track from its mailer, toss the cartridge in his car, go off on his route, and deliver, *delivered*, the empty box! An eight track! It wasn't even a cassette! It was an old eight track! Then, when the lady came in the Post Office screaming, "He did it! He did it! I know he did it!" the carrier lies his head off!"

"How'd she know?" Rick asked, swallowing back a laugh.

"She didn't, not really. She figured he was the last to handle it, so . . . it didn't really matter though. She was fuming; she was going to blame somebody! All the while the two of them are going at it, I'm in my cubicle listening, thinking, *'She's right! You're making a good hourly solely for your honesty and, for a moment, your not. She's got you dead to rights! Now, give her the tape and back away from the stamps. You're fired!'*" Rick laughed, a half toke choke. "Funny? Stupid, if you ask me."

"What? It was just a tape."

"Then two, three weeks ago, I'm out on the road on this route when, while mowing his lawn, some old guy has a heart attack. He tumbles down the embankment separating his property from his neighbor, lands in a stream, lawnmower and all. His neighbor, a Metro cop, *a cop*, comes racing out his front door, arms flailing, to get my attention. I pulled over, ran down the embankment into the stream, and found him giving the old guy mouth-to-mouth. The cop's turning green, about to blow lunch, when he tells me to do it 'cause it's making him sick! He's a cop; he saves lives for a living! I deliver junk mail! I end up giving the old guy mouth-to-mouth for, I don't know, two, three minutes, while the cop did chest compressions." Rick stared at me with the stupidest grin, then sparked another. "Give me that!"

"So, how's the old guy?"

"Dead. He was dead when he landed, that's what the Postmaster told me."

"How'd he know?"

"The cop called, told the Postmaster what happened. Guess what he said?"

"Who?"

"The Postmaster! Does short term memory loss mean anything to you?"

"What'd he say?"

"People die every day!"

"See, I told you!" Rick howled, laughing 'til he choked. "And?"

"And, that was it! That's *all* he said! This sucks!"

"What sucks?"

"Life sucks!"

"Well, yeah, if that's the way you want to look at it. It's what you make of it. Doesn't matter what you do. You still have to deal with it."

"Right, but that's just it. What you just said. 'It's what you make of it.' I can cope; deal with it when I have to, but not here, not like this, not anymore. Something has to change. There's more, there has to be." I was hedging, leading him in. I had something on my mind, but I wasn't quite sure how to go about bringing it up. "Let me ask you something. Do you intend to spend the next twenty, thirty, however many years, your working life, doing whatever it is boilermakers do?"

Rick shrugged. "Yeah, I can see that."

"Really?" I wasn't at all surprised at his answer, just taken back a bit at his seeming passive attitude toward time, toward a lifetime. "Well, if that's what you want, that's good. For me, I don't think sorting junk mail is enough to go on."

"You're gonna blow it. Don't blow it."

"Whattya mean, 'Don't blow it?'" Only way I'd 'blow it' is if I won." *That should do it. Here we go!'*

"Won what?" Rick asked. *'Can I call 'em or what?'*

Now that I was finally getting it out, I had to smile. "If I won next month."

"The hell you talking about?"

"Ever heard of a restaurant, 'The Golden Pheasant'?"

"Pheasant? I've heard Rooster. I think its Golden Rooster."

"Pheasant. Anyway, there's going to be a show, sort of a competition, there."

"Talent show?"

"Competition."

"Whatever. So?"

"I'm in it."

"In what?" he asked, lost in his eternal haze, earnestly dumbfounded.

"It! The show! I'm an entry! Geezus, you ever think of giving that stuff up for Lent?"

Choking on a hanging smoke cloud, he finally asked, "What're you going to do?"

"Have another. Here's the thing; win, and a Finals invite is automatic, but even if you don't, if the Judges' are impressed, they can *put* you in the Finals."

"Where?"

"Where what?"

"Where are the Finals?"

I had to grin. "New York City."

"When?"

"Two, three months. November, December, something like that."

"What for? I mean, what's the big deal?"

"Ready? A full scholarship to the *New York Academy of Theatre Arts*," I heard myself crow. It just rolled out, 'smooth as 'butta', as they say. The title had a certain 'far away from here' dream sound to it. I think he got the idea.

Rick choked. "You're shittin'?" His reaction told me he had.

"Pretty impressive, eh?"

"Don't mean a thing to me," he said, with a huge grin, "but it sure sounded good!" Laughing, coughing, he rose to leave.

"You know, you can be a real smart ass when you want to."

"Yeah, I know. It's a gift." Fishing in his Marlboro pack, he dropped a pinner on the table.

"Here, all yours."

"I'll just suck off the cloud awhile."

I heard him say, "Don't blow it," as the backdoor slammed.

I slid open the side window as he walked past. "Hey, Rick, you say it like you think I have a chance to pull this off."

"I don't know. You haven't said what you're going to do. Shirley says you can't dance."

"What does your sister know? We went out on one date, to dinner, no dancing."

"Oh. Well, you don't play the guitar or anyth—"

"No."

"Well, that pretty much . . . you a ventriloquist?" We laughed.

"No."

"Magic?

"I write."

"Yeah? Can you sing?"

"No. I don't have to."

"Whattya mean you don't have to? What're you gonna do? Yodel?"

"I'm going to tell a story."

This was the last, the absolute furthest thing he expected to hear. When he finally spoke all he said was, "Funny?"

"Huh?"

"I'm just saying, it better be funny."

"No, actually it's more a drama."

"I take it back."

"Take what back?"

"You ain't gonna blow it." I heard him chuckle, as he shuffled away.

~~~

One month later.

Rick eyed the items I readied to take to the show. "Where'd you get the stuff?"

"The pajamas my dad gave me for Christmas, awhile ago. The cane came from—"

"It's okay, I guess, but why'd he get you pajamas for Christmas?"

"Why? Well, first off, he didn't *get* them for me, he *gave* them to me, and second, I get your drift, but why not? At the time, I thought they were a good change from *another trunk load of paint-by-numbers. Never mind, it's a long story. The cane belonged to my grandfather. The side table I pulled from the attic. This is my old nasty bathrobe, and a picture frame to put on the table."

"Who's in the picture?"

"Your sister. Naked." Rick grabbed the frame. "Calm down. There's nobody in it."

"Where'd you get the rocking chair?"

"Cool, huh? I got it from Mr. Hudgins, four houses down."

"The guy who's always sitting on his front porch?"

"Same."

"Rocking?"

"Not anymore," I said, matter-of-factly.

"You stole the old guy's rocker? You can't steal—"

"I told him what I was doing, I asked, and he lent it to me."

With an odd look, "Oh," was all Rick said.

"What?"

"What the hell are you doing, anyway?"

"I told you. I'm going to tell a story. You'll see tonight. You're still going, right?"

"Yeah, me and the girlfriend."

"Maureen? You two back together?"

"We're good. The 'Exorcist' opened last week. I took her to see it."

"What'd she say?"

"She thought it was scary."

"No, I mean about tonight?"

"Oh, she thinks you're scary, too."

"'xcuse me?"

"Well, she laughed, but she knows you, so . . . what'd you expect?"

"Anybody else know?"

"I didn't tell anybody." He broke out a bag and started rolling.

"Good."

"But, she might've."

"You're kidding, right?"

"We'll all vote for you."

"What if I bomb?"

"So? Don't."

"Easier said than done."

"You're getting up in front of a bunch of strangers, dressed like an old guy, telling a story nobodies ever heard. Do you really think you're gonna win?"

"What do you think?"

"Of what?"

"The concept."

"Concept? I think you're gonna need all the votes you can get!"

(ring) "Hello. Hey, Jodi. Yeah, pheasant. Golden Pheasant. About eight."

"Rooster."

"Jodi, yeah, it might be Rooster. Don't know. It's a small town. You'll find . . . eight . . . bye."

"Who was that?"

"Jodi," thinking, "I don't know, something or other. She's doing my make-up."

Rick gagged, coughing on a long, deep toke. *"Doing your what?"*

"I hope boilermakers make good money, 'cause that's just a waste of good herb! C'mon, help me load the car."

* . . . *another trunk load of paint-by-numbers.'* See novel, *'Never Play Leapfrog with a Unicorn'*.

~2~

Looking for Neon

The venue looked nothing like I'd imagined, yet everything I expected. Simply put, the 'Golden Rooster' was your typical, any small town USA restaurant, changing owners and names as often as the daily specials. This month—Chinese cuisine, featuring cocktails served with multi-colored paper umbrellas.

I barely spotted Rick, standing off in the shadows of the overflow parking lot. "Told ya!" He beamed, pointing to the orange neon.

"Point for you. Where's your girlfriend?"

"Who?"

"Maureen? The girlfriend? She here?"

"Here?" He paused. "Oh, here! No. She's inside." *'Now how do I respond to that?'* "The place is packed! There's a ton of rug-rats."

"Let's start over. Focus. What are you doing out here?"

"Had some business to take care of."

"Visine's in the glove compartment."

"I saw your friends, Dean and Loretta, inside."

"You did? Excellent. They're the only ones I told, well, besides you."

"And there's—"

"And there's . . . what?"

"And there's a whole lot of other people you know." I couldn't help but glare at him. "I know, I know, but Maureen mentioned it to this one, this one told that one, that one told anoth—"

"I've never done this in front of people before. Does that ring a bell?"

"So you said."

"One time in front of strangers! If I go down in flames, big deal, nobody knows me, I gave it a shot. But now, I tell you, I'm nervous as hell!"

"So, now you go down in flames in front of strangers, and suck the big one in front of your friends!" Rick laughed, Visine streaking down his face. "Be like killing two birds with one stone."

"You're really getting on my nerves."

"Yeah, it's—"

"A gift, I know. Do me a favor, shut-up!" I was joking, though rattled at what lay ahead.

"Want a hand lugging the stuff in?"

"No, not yet. I want to see what it's all about."

~~~

Entering through the second set of doors, I was greeted by a massive bar. Every brand, every type of liquor imaginable lined the island's endless length, three tiers high, right down the middle. There had to be seating for thirty-plus patrons. Friends, acquaintances, some I had not seen since I can't remember when, took up at least half the seats.

I walked right into it.

They whooped and shrieked, toasting me like a long lost sailor at sea. An eclectic lot to be sure, most in their early and mid-twenties. I put on a good front, waving, nodding, smiling, though what I really wanted, for both me and them, was for all of them to disappear. *'Too late now. If nothing goes wrong, this will be a night to remember.'*

Somehow, a Monarch butterfly had been born in the pit of my stomach, and wanted out.

Behind the bar, a single row of dining booths lined the back wall, a number of small cocktail tables in front. More booths lined the far left and right walls, with more free-standing tables. In the main dining room's center, a clear, open wood floor where, normally, patrons could dance. Two long tables were set, one at the head of the cleared floor space, for the judges, and another at the far end wall, which held a good number of identical trophies. Centered in front of the generic trophy table, set on rich red fabric, standing at least three feet tall, stood one very ornate trophy. This had to be the First Place trophy.

Going one step further to explain, I had never competed, presented, staged, or let but few read my scribblings, my stories. Winning that garish trophy would give one person, one attempt, one entry, validation, which meant, now, I wanted to win. Because I wanted the trophy? No. Because I needed the trophy? No, well, yes, sort of. I needed it for what it stood for; one entry presented here tonight was the best in the house. Now, not only did I want to be invited to the finals in New York, I wanted to take that garish Grand Trophy home.

Rick came over, pointing across the room. "See the woman at the Judges table? She wants to see you. You have to sign-in."

"What are the odds I take that home with me tonight?"

"Really? She's old! I mean really, really old! Wait 'til you get closer before you deci—"

"I mean, the trophy!"

"Oh. If I were betting, I'd say you have a snowball's chance in hell."

'When the odds are stacked against you, there's nothing like a friend's encouraging words.'

~~~

"Okay, you're all signed in. That'll be ten dollars. Registration fee," said the woman at the Judges table.

"Is there a sound system available? I have pre-recorded music, on cassette."

"For?"

"Background."

"Oh, to sing to. Let's see," she said, checking my sign-up info. "You checked off Adult Category, but, oh, here we are. You forgot to check 'singer'. How will we introduce you properly if you don't fill out everything?"

"I'm not."

"Not? Not what?"

"A singer."

"Oh, a dancer. There, you should have checked off danc—"

I smiled at the thought. "No, I don't dance. That's not right either. I'm telling a story."

"Oh, and what is your story about?"

"About three minutes."

"You're a comedian?"

"No."

"An actor then?"

"Well, I don't . . . thank you, but no."

"I have to check off something."

"I want to be a writer."

"That's not on the list."

"Then, storyteller."

She set the clipboard down. "Describe to me, tell me a little about your story."

"Well, it's nothing you've heard. I mean, it's mine. I wrote it. I think if I were to describe it, it's like a mini-theatre scene."

"Oh, isn't that interesting. A story about mini-theatre. I've never heard of such a thing."

"No, it isn't *about* mini-theatre. I just made that up. Maybe the judges will give me an extra point for originality."

"Maybe. That will be ten dollars."

'If I can't explain what I'm doing, how can I expect people to understand what I'm doing?'

~~~

15

"Shirley's here," Rick said, "she said to say, 'Hi'. He grinned. "Hi."

"Why?"

"Why what?"

"Why is she here?"

"I don't know. She stops and gawks at car accidents, too."

"Thanks, that helps a lot. Again, why is she here?"

"What'd I just say?"

"Did your straight man die? Where is she?"

"In the corner booth."

"Which corner booth?" I asked, peering through the smoke, squinting through the shadows. "I don't see . . . who's that? I see a . . . Raymond? Is that Raymond? Is she back with him?"

"Who knows?"

"I still don't see her? Where is she?"

"She's there."

"Where? Under him?"

"Hey, that's my sister!"

"What? Suddenly you're Prince Valiant?"

"She wanted to show her support."

"Horizontally?"

"Look, she's here. He's here. It's done." Rick shrugged. "It's a good thing."

"And, how's that?"

"Two more votes." He laughed.

"It's like I'm on a toboggan speeding straight to hell!" I said, shaking my head.

"So relax and enjoy the ride."

"Easier said—"

Glancing over my shoulder, Rick cut me off. "Don't turn around!" he warned. So, of course, I started to turn. "I said, don't! What the hell is that?"

Out of the corner of my eye, I spotted the cause of Rick's alarm. "Jodi," I called out.

"What the hell happened to her face?"

"She's into make-up. She's a make-up artist. Get it?"

"If I were a brain surgeon I wouldn't operate on myself."

"That's somewhat reassuring."

"Meaning?"

"I think you'd be disappointed at what little you'd find."

"Here she comes. When you're ready, I'll be at the bar."

"Who's that?" Jodi asked.

"A friend of mine . . . Rick."

"Cute." She grinned.

"You're not going to believe this, but he just said the same about you."

"Really?" she gushed, flapping her long, deep blue colored lashes, and severe to a taper, dramatically drawn, black to blonde eyebrows. I hate to say it but, with all her make-up, she was hard to look at.

"Yeah, but he's got the girlfriend and all."

"You say that like it's a bad thing. I'm thinking week-end, not lifetime!"

"Oh." I laughed. "Well, no offense, but I think you have a few years on him."

"What are you trying to say? I'd be easy on him!"

"I never realized you were so—"

"So, what?"

"Frisky!"

"What's wrong with frisky? Frisky's good."

"Yeah, if you're a cat."

"Funny," she groaned. "Okay, enough of this already. Where's the make-up area?"

"Wherever we make one." Jodi rolled her eyes. "Think of it as off-off Broadway."

"Off-off, off-off, off . . ."

~~~

The sounds 'tap . . . tap-tap' then, "One, two . . . one, two. We on?" were followed by a sharp microphone squeal. "Good evening everyone. Welcome to Talent USA East compete—"

Jodi nudged me. "What's it called?"

"Community Auditions," I joked.

"Huh?"

"Do you remember Ted Mack's Original Amateur Hour?" Jodi chuckled, nudging me again, harder.

"As you know, for months now, a series of competitions have been taking place all over the East coast in search of the best, the brightest, the stars of tomor—"

"What am I doing?" I whispered to Jodi.

"What?"

"What the hell am I—"

"Having a nervous breakdown," she quipped, a toothy smile flashed from her big red lips.

"I'm past that. I'm going for full meltdown."

"By the way, what *are* you doing?"

"That seems to be the question of the night."

"Over a period of four days, from Thursday, November seventh, to the Grand Award ceremonies Sunday evening, November tenth, winners, and invited hopefuls from local competitions, will gather at the Biltmore Hotel in New York City to compete once again. Judges for the New York pageant will be drawn from a pool of directors, choreographers, talent agents, publicists . . . personalities from every spectrum of the entertainment industry."

Looking about the room, except for the pocket of people who knew me and why I was there, I was not any different from anyone else. *'Why can't I leave well enough alone?'* I had heard enough from the host and from me. I felt like I was going to be sick. I knew I was going to be sick.

"Where are you going?" asked Jodi.

"Home." I smiled, making my way out to the parking lot.

~~~

19

"I saw you leave. Figured you were ready to bring the stuff in," Rick said, as I wretched in the bushes. "You okay?"

"Something didn't agree with me."

"What? Show biz?"

"Hundreds of comics looking for work and I'm here with Wally one-liner!"

"It's about to get worse."

"Really? I don't see how that's—"

"Hey, guys," Raymond said, his beer barrel chest underscored by his Coors Mountain belly. "So, now you're an actor, eh?"

"What're you talking about?"

"The woman, the host, read the line-ups in the different categories. You're with four others in the adult part. A comic, three singing acts, and an actor."

"Process of elimination," Rick concluded, with a grin.

"Oh, and you're last."

"Last is good," I said, more to reassure myself.

"Could be, then again, it could be a sign."

"Sign of what?" As soon as I said it, I knew I had set myself up in Raymond's sights.

"You know; Dead End, Do Not Enter, No Adm—"

"Oh." I interrupted Raymond's laugh, playing dumb. "I don't get it."

"And you never will! See ya inside, thespian. This oughta be good!" He made a noise, a snaggletooth laugh, as he turned, walking away.

"Hey, my sister's no lesbian!"

"Thespian! Thes . . . an actor! What're you talking about? He never said—"

"Hey, it's a joke. Calm down."

"When he said I'd never get it, was he referring to Shirley? What an ass! A total ass!"

"Yeah, well, when you have his money, you can get anything."

"Even your sister?"

"Look at her. Why do you think she's with him and not with you?"

"Really? What'd she say? 'Cause I thought she had a good time when we went out. I know I did. I never understood why she never called me back, why we never went out again."

"She's known him, dated him, since high school . . . way before he took over his family's landscaping business. He came around the day after you two went out. Money talks."

A burst of applause, loud and growing louder, broke the quiet of the parking lot.

Pointing to the restaurant, to a large window where lights shone bright on the main floor, "Look at all those kids!" Rick exclaimed. "There's gotta be thirty of them!" We watched as they filed off the main floor, laughed as a new crew of kids filed back on.

"Just those two groups of rug-rats alone, at ten dollars a pop, six hundred in entry fees."

"Six ten," he said, nodding to me. "What a scam. Ready to bring the stuff in?"

21

"Yeah, but we need one person to . . . Dean," I called out. About to enter the building, I spotted his trademark reddish-orange afro. Dean heard me yell, turned, and walked toward us. "How's it going?"

"Working more, enjoying it less." In his late twenties, an electrician by trade, Dean volunteered his services to area community theatres. Well, no, 'volunteered' might be too generous a word; he did lighting per Loretta's, his actress girlfriend, insistence. That's how we met. I had been in my first stage production; Cole Porters 'Anything Goes'. Dean did lights, Loretta was the female lead, I was a character extra.

"Dean, this is Rick. Rick, meet—"

"We're old buddies," Dean said. "I dated Shirley, his sister." I burst out in laughter, shaking my head.

"I thought you looked familiar!" Rick exclaimed, a moment of clarity breaking through the haze.

Dean looked at me. "What's so funny?"

"Nothing, inside joke. Can I ask a favor?"

"Ask away, but I ain't leaving, not 'til you do your . . . you know."

"Stay, stay. I'm glad you're here. This is what I need. There are three categories; Kids, Teens, and Adults. There are five entries in the Adult Category. I'm on last, the very last of the night. When the fourth entry finishes, when they walk off, I need you guys to center the rocker on the floor, but back about five feet. I think everyone sitting on the sidelines will be able to see then. Facing the chair, hook the cane over the back left hand corner, set the table on the right side. I taped a doily to the table top, smooth it out so the edging hangs over, then stand the picture up at an angle facing the chair. What else? I think that's it. Am I forgetting anything?"

"Seeing no one knows what you're doing, we can't be much help."

"Good point," Rick chimed in. I had to laugh, knowing they were right.

"Place the stuff as I told you, that alone is help enough." I looked at them for a hint of either being unclear of the instructions given. "You guys good? You sure?"

"Aye, aye, Admiral," Dean joked, hoisting the rocker over his head. Rick hooked the cane over a shoulder, took the side table in one hand, picture frame in the other.

"Break a leg," they said in unison, laughing, walking away.

"See you inside. Don't forget to angle the frame. Oh, and tell Jodi to meet me by the doors."

Alone in the shadows, on this unseasonably warm September night, I tried to relax. I had an odd feeling in the pit of my stomach.

It felt as if my Monarch butterfly had given birth.

To twins!

~3~

Paint. Powder. No Miracles!

Jodi had set up shop out of the way, along the rear wall, behind the last booth. "You asked me to 'bring old'," she said, emptying her make-up bag. "I brought what I think you'll need. How old do you want to go? Forty? Sixty?"

"Have you ever done older?"

"No, but for the right amount," she winked, "I could be persuaded," and tittered.

"I mean old. Eighty, eighty-five?"

"I wouldn't go that old for any amount of money!" She laughed, blurting, "Groucho Marx!"

"You really should meet Rick. I think you two would hit it off."

"You think? So, what's it going to be?"

"Huh?" I scowled.

"Really? You're serious? Eighty-five?"

"Do eighty-four and a half, I'll be happy."

"Then be happy." She smiled, as she set to creating. Moving about my face with an artist's intent, lining, smudging, blotting, and sponging, I had to grin. I knew I was her guinea pig. She was in uncharted waters. Hell, we were in the same boat, for that matter! *'She's the artist, my face her canvas. How theatrical, how dramatic is that?'* I laughed. "Something funny?"

"No, nothing," I lied.

"Relax," she suggested, as I squirmed, searching for comfort. She stopped. "Have you ever been made-up before?"

"Yeah, when we met. You did make-up for—"

"'Anything Goes', I know. That was a powder wipe to offset the lights. Besides that?"

"When I was a kid, I was in make-up for a dance recital."

"You were in a dance recital?"

"No, but I was made-up for one. It's a long story."

"Curious. Aside from your 'Anything Goes' walk-on, what else have you done?"

"Where?"

"Anywhere. I mean, besides community theatre."

"Done? What?"

"Roles? Stage work? Film?"

"Oh, so far, that's been it."

"High school?"

"No. They wouldn't let me act on stage. I was told I acted up enough in class. Bit of a catch twenty-two don't you think?"

Finally, after a deafening pause, she asked, "Where did you rehearse for this?"

"This?"

"Tonight."

"Oh, in my living room."

"Your living room. That's it?"

"No, the shower, too. Great acoustics."

"And?"

"And, I used a Right Guard can for a microphone." Jodi's smile was tinged with caution, apprehension. I knew what she was getting at, but I did not have the answer she was looking for. In my way of thinking, *'You have to start somewhere,'* and the Golden Rooster was as good a place as any. After a long pause, "You don't quite know what to make of this, of tonight, do you? It's okay. Nobody else does either, including me!" We shared a laugh. "Why do you think I asked you; called on you specifically?"

"Because I'm the only make-up person you know?"

"True, but even though you told me you've never gone this old before, there's a big part of me trusting you can, without making me look the fool. Of course, there's a very good chance I'll take care of that all by myself, when I get out there!" Jodi smiled. "And that 'walk-on' as you call it, turned a pretty good review for my first time out. I quote, *'As a love struck sailor he was silly, but cute, dancing, improvising with a mop, behind a morbid duet.'* Because of that one

27

show I met a ton of good people, present company included." I think she blushed, but behind all her make-up, I couldn't tell.

"Speaking of which, Dean and Loretta are here. Did you see them?"

"I did."

"I learned a number of things from that show. First, I could have done without 'cute' in the review. Second, I can't dance, though I knew this early on. And, I can't sing. Well, I could once, a little, then Janis Joplin came along with 'Piece of My Heart'. Singing along to that a few hundred times, volume blaring, will ruin anybody's voice," I chuckled. "And last of all, I loved it."

"Loved what?"

"The stage. The audience."

"I thought," she started, "I mean . . ." then stopped.

"What? You thought what?"

"I thought . . . aren't you the one who said you didn't like people?"

"What? No! What I said was, 'I love audiences. I can't stand people!' It's a joke. You can't have one without the other."

"Have you been watching old Mickey Rooney movies?"

"Good one. No, but you know, when I was a kid, I'd look over the TV Guide for the entire week, and if I saw a Cagney or Rooney movie listed for the noontime film, I'd pretend I was sick so I could stay home from school." There was a long pause. "Where were we going with this?"

"I forget. Oh, so no one has ever seen, I mean, you've never done this before?"

"No." There was a long, awkward silence. "You ever done eighty-five before?" Jodi had a little grin. "Sound familiar?"

"Close your eyes," she said, going back to her canvas. "Think happy thoughts."

The thought, *'I'm last',* made me happy.

~~~

On the main floor, one Kid's Category dance troupe followed another, as they took a shot at putting their best foot forward. At ten dollars a head, you didn't have to be a math wiz to figure out somebody was making some serious cash.

Finally, many sign-up fees later, the Kid's Category came to an end. Then, much to my personal delight, to calm the mob of kids and their giddy anticipation, plus clear the room of them early, the Judges announced the Kid's Category winner. The delight heard in the high, sharp, trebled pitch of their glee could have, I'm positive, cracked some unsuspecting soul's glass eye! If, by odd chance, the eye remained intact once the din subsided, lady luck was short lived. This pitch was surpassed (much to the dismay of every nerve ending in my being) when the Judges further delighted the room with the announcement, "Every Kid's Category entry is invited to compete in New York". The squeals went right through me.

In a flash of crystal clarity the moneymaking means of this machine lay wide open! Somehow I knew, come New York, there would again be entry fees, plus a glossy program with all entrant's headshots posted at a charge, and whatever else the brain trust could think up to make a buck. At once, I felt like I'd been tricked, foolish for being drawn in. I felt stupid because my friends could see what was going on and, for the reason they were here, me, I was humiliated, and I hadn't even done anything yet!

There could have been any number of entries in the Teen Category, but I really could not, for love or money, say how many. I never heard a song sung, a note hit, or a single round of applause. As I sat there, head back, eyes closed, as Jodi touched and fussed, the realization of the organizer's squirrelly, mischievous ways, rattled me to the core and slowly ate at me. I was now more disgusted than nervous. I wanted out. I wished to vanish; wanted to disappear. But, as much as I wanted to walk away, end this, for one inexplicable reason or other, I simply couldn't.

'Go!'

I wasn't glued to the chair; my feet were not bolted to the floor.

'Now!'

As bitter as I was at the moment, why I didn't get up and leave, I couldn't understand. Soon I'd discover why and, in doing, scare the living hell out of myself . . . all by myself!

~~~

The first entry was a comic. A comedian? Well, you be the judge. His opening line was memorable; that is, it stuck in the crevice of my mind, where all sorts of useless debris take refuge forever and ever.

"What's with SUBARU? When I pull up behind one, I know what it is, it says so, SUBARU. But when I spot one in my rearview, coming up behind me, I don't see SUBARU . . . no . . . I see . . . U-R-A-BUS! So, what is it? A car . . . or . . . a bus?"

That's it! I kid you not! That was his opener! The sad part? The even sadder part? This was his funniest bit! I don't recall any more of his material, but I clearly remember it just got worse, and worse, and wor . . . the funny part? They loved him! He was one of those big, lanky, every office, every machine shop, everyday, everywhere kind of guys. Once his minor lackings were excused, i.e., stage presence, material, and the grating tic of stepping on his own punch lines with his own laughter, to be fair, you couldn't help but love the guy.

And this bothered me.

I didn't mind the thought of losing, well I did, but I wanted, needed to lose to somebody respectful, as opposed to an entry who won, who stole the night on the good guy pity vote. I know that's harsh, but he was not funny! If it makes any sense, if I must lose, I was hoping it would be to someone who could show me, through some honed, polished, not to leave out God-given creative ability, why I shouldn't be here.

Entry number two; a duet in their mid-twenties. The lyrics portrayed them as hopeless, lovelorn, WWII dockside romantics, bidding tearful, hanky waving, off-to-the-front good-byes. As stated, the lyrics portrayed them as such. What they portrayed was something entirely different.

She was, if not six-foot tall, pretty darn close, rail skinny, with a long, thin nose, which pinched her eyes together. Her nose reminded me of a bird's beak.

The doughboy was short, quite a bit shorter than her. He was stubby in build with a most annoying, over-the-top, mugging habit. Their intertwined solos were done well, but as a twosome they couldn't hit, let alone carry, a note in a bucket!

Entry three was a singer on crutches, left leg in a cast, right arm in a sling. She'd been sent home from the hospital that afternoon, after a car mishap two days prior. Understandably, she was a wreck, nervous and otherwise.

Entry four was . . . that son-of-a-bitch Raymond lied! Entry four was *me!*

As a final touch, with a can of silver/white hair color, Jodi had begun spraying my hair back to front. Hearing my name announced, I startled, jumping up! Not realizing a large patch of the back and crown, one-third of my head, was now silver/white, while the sides and front were still naturally black, I proceeded to weave through the crowd heading for the Judges table. It was not until I glanced at my reflection in the window that I saw the aged six-foot skunk! A few people gasped, some laughed, others mildly shrieked.

As if my being caught off-guard was not disruption enough, Dean and Rick jumped into action doing a very good Keystone bumbling Cops impression! Looking across the open floor, *"Watch your heads!"* into the audience, *"Coming through!"* at first I saw the rocking chair gliding above the heads of the crowd, *"Move!"* then disappear, *"Watch out!"* followed by a loud crash, *"Ah, shit!"* yelling, laughing, and applause! The house lights came up.

To any sympathetic ear at the Judge's table, I blathered, meekly pleaded, "I thought I was . . . I wasn't . . . I'm not ready. It came too fast!"

"You sound like a frustrated virgin!"

Knowing the voice all too well I turned, scanning the crowd and spotting him, "You finished?"

"On her wedding night!" Raymond glanced at Shirley for a smile of wise-ass support. He pulled her to him as the laughter spread. With much difficulty, I struggled to dismiss the overwhelming notion of running both their bodies through an industrial wood chipper!

Though the brunt of Raymond's joke, I wanted to laugh, too. That is, I wanted to, but I couldn't. Not with Raymond. Not at that. Not until I heard a most grating, snorting, nervous, noisy excuse for a laugh did I finally join in. It was Shirley who possessed the hideous laugh! I had never heard a female, let alone another human being, make such a piggish noise! I had finally found the wrinkle, the hairline crack in God's blue-eyed, rose petal soft, gift to mankind! For me, finding the flaw meant re-discovering the joy of sleep, of peace of mind. No longer would I lie awake nights fantasizing, lose waking hours daydreaming about her. I'd found a flaw and the flaw shall set me free!

'Any drowning animal, sucking nothing but water, will grasp at anything, even another's misfortune, to get buoyant!'

Turning back, the four Judges conferred with a very short, plump, ageless man, with thinning, slicked back black hair, and a blemish free, colorless face. He wore white loafers and orange casual slacks, neat and creased. A plaid sports coat topped his white dress shirt and, hanging just over his belly, sticking out at least five inches from contact with his white belt, a loud, broad Hawaiian tie. I found it oddly amusing how this washed-out, lily white ball of dough, the one person who could reap the benefits of five minutes in the sun, would be wearing a Hawaiian tie!

"Ladies and gentlemen, if I could I have your attention; a change in order. For voting purposes, please make note. Entry five will now be entry four; entry four is now entry five," the older female Judge announced. Another Judge, a bit perturbed at the switch, judging from his animated, arm-waving, finger pointing manner, was making a mountain out of a molehill at the chaos moments earlier. Judge number three, a female, tried calming him, while the fourth Judge, a male, sat, arms folded, totally removed, oblivious to what all.

The unassuming man took his place at the microphone. "Entry number four," read the mentally absent Judge, "Mr. Cellophane."

'Wha . . . excuse me? Mister . . . ?' I thought, questioning my hearing. Like wildfire, the room went from a loud murmur to flat out giggles and titters.

Made aware of his error, the Judge re-read. It seems the entrant's name was Harold, Harold something or other, not Mr. Cellophane. The song's title was 'Mr. Cellophane'. As I turned, retreating back to Jodi, the houselights dimmed. Harold's pre-recorded music began.

The spray cloud of hair coloring grew, as did a gathering crowd of curious on lookers. While Jodi sprayed away, I sat, trying to listen to Harold. I think his song had to do with people who spend their lives being looked right through, not being seen, never being heard. It's hard to say. From my angle he was hard to see and, with all the chatter, I didn't hear a word.

Running out of time, I threw the robe on over my T-shirt. Hiding behind the last booth, I dropped my jeans, slipped on the pajama bottoms, and stepped into a pair of waiting slippers. Jodi gave one last look of approval.

The smattering of applause told me Harold's song was over. I was about to thank Jodi for all her help, when she lit up, saying something about 'luck'. She reached in her bag, taking out, handing me a small box, "Should I open it now?"

"For luck." I heard a subtle hint of 'now's a good a time as any' in her voice.

"I thought wishing someone 'good luck' before going on was a bad thing?"

"I'm not wishing you luck, I'm giving you luck. There's a difference . . . I hope."

Opening the box, I found a shiny, odd shaped gold piece and neck chain. Knowing what to say was easy, "Thank-you". Knowing what I held in my hand, what I was thanking her for, was a bit more difficult. "Jodi . . . this is . . . I don't know what . . . I . . ." I hadn't a clue.

"It's an Italian horn."

"Ah."

"Our fifth and final entry of the night, if he's ready. Is he ready?" prompted the Judge.

Jodi took the gift, "I'll hold it for you. Go! Go! Go!"

"It's very nice. It really is. Hey, if this works, if the luck rubs off, would you go to New York?"

Jodi smiled. She looked past the old made-up canvas, "Maybe," into my eyes. "We'll see." It was a one-pulse moment, meant for the fleet of heart, not the weak. There was a near invisible move forward by us both. It was then I noticed, really noticed for the first time, just how many shades, tones, and colors she wore on her face. And, just how shiny, just how clear I could see myself in those big red lips! And, just how much clowns scare me!

To cover an awkward moment, I asked, "How do I look?"

34

"You should be so blessed in sixty years." She laughed. "You better get out there."

Funny how missed moments, words, touches, a kiss, how a single kiss missed, will haunt you. Even then, I knew there'd be times, many times, when that kiss would be welcome.

I turned and began walking the restaurant's length. I strode into, through, and past, a bevy of tipsy friends, a few drunken acquaintances, and a throng of strangers with even stranger smiling stares. Oh, and one still grumpy, unforgiving Judge who, when I walked past, I swear, sneered at me. *'Twittlehead! Get over it!'*

I made my way along the far wall, amidst and among the last stretch of gawking, jostling, audience members. Most of them needed, had to get, an up close and personal eyeful of this most bizarre made-up sight. Pausing, I watched Rick and Dean, like dues paying union stagehands, set the scene up. Patiently, I waited for them to clear from the floor area.

Unexpected and gentle, a hand slid across the back, the neck area of my natty, faded, blue terry cloth robe. I did not startle or duck away; rather, I stood motionless, as fingers circled around revealing an arm, a body, a smile. *'Shirley?'*

Her hand slid down the robe's front, stopping at the rip, the wound, the tear, the gaping gash, which ran from the right underarm seam down at an angle, halfway across my chest.

"Character effect." I chuckled.

Her eyes sparkled back, her index and middle finger gliding under the terry cloth, into the hole. Through my T-shirt I felt her fingernails make small circles about my nipple. "Is your character affected?" she asked, with an impish grin.

I gave a quick glance about; Raymond was nowhere to be seen. I leaned over, whispering, "I really don't think these folks expect an aroused old man."

"Is this all it takes to arouse an old man?" she asked. Not missing a beat, her fingers were out of the hole, her hand now set on the side of my neck. With minimum 'come here' pull and forward motion, hidden in half lit shadows, surrounded by a wall of strangers, she directed my mouth to hers and kissed me in a way Raymond would never know.

Gentle.

Or ever miss.

Tender.

Or appreciate.

I caught the whisper of butter rum Life Saver.

I was afloat in my very own blissful abyss. I vow to you here and now, not only did I feel her temperature rise, I felt my heart skip a beat. In due time, I swear to God, I heard her eyelids open. Time moved slow, in slowest of slow motion, as my eyelids cracked open. For a half second we were eyeball to eyeball, then Shirley's look darted over my right shoulder, her eyes fixed, staring. Reacting quick was not an option as my heart was doing a double-back flip, while my mind, a holding cell of erratic common sense, tried convincing my blood flow to redirect!

Turning, looking about as fast, as best I could, I saw Dean and Rick heading off in one direction. Harold went by me with a wink and a nod. Raymond was coming straight for us, but was looking down, apparently trying to close his zipper, and that, along with a couple hundred voyeurs, was everyone.

Everyone that is, but Jodi, who, I somehow knew, had seen everything. She made few friends as she bulled through the crowd, steps heavy and rushed, making her way back to the other side of the room.

"Blue robe, green T-shirt, brown pajama bottoms, whatever color slippers," Raymond listed, a little too loud. "Wardrobe!" he bellowed, snapping his fingers. Laughter rang.

"Who dresses you?" chided Shirley, the twinkle in her eye gone behind a stolen wink.

"That's my girl!" Raymond announced, pulling Shirley to him, wink unseen.

As I turned away, "Break a leg!" said Shirley.

"Bust a gasket!" Raymond razzed, again to more laughter.

In my peripheral vision I saw the Judges watching, staring, following me. Three seemed humored at this rag-tag sight. The twittlehead Judge, the one who I believe sneered at me, now seemed to be glowering.

In the last two minutes I had felt my heart soar then crash land, the earth move then abruptly stop, any positive energy in the room become disrupted. The walk to the rocker seemed a never-ending journey. All I wanted was to sit down.

The idea of having an audience, to find out once and for all whether this would work, was finally about to happen. The thought of this moment, which both entertained and caused me heart palpitations for the last month, was now at hand.

I loved it.

I hated it.

I embraced it.

I despised it.

'It's Showtime!'

~4~

Mr. Twittlehead

I settled in, gently rocking. *I'm sitting. I'm safe. I'm okay. That should be worth an extra point or two.'* I smiled inward. Then I made the mistake of looking up, taking it all in. Everyone seemed to be grinning.

Then I heard the first titter, the fourth, then the twelfth, then . . . it skittered through the room like an erratic Chinese bottle rocket. On the surface this would have been a good sign . . . had it been a comedy club!

They were nervous titters, those were edgy smiles. Had I a way of gauging them individually, I know I would have found a handful to be somewhat leery of what was to come, that is, more leery than I . . . and I knew what was coming!

I shifted in the rocker to steal another look. *'Oh God, what have I . . . figure it out . . . figu . . . '* This audience, these people, whether here to support a friend, relative, or neighbor, are here because they each want to leave with something none of them had walking in. They were looking for the, 'I wasn't expecting *that* singer, *that* act, *that* person', surprise. They want to be touched, moved. They want to be reminded to breathe. They want a rush so powerful their neck hairs tingle! *'Whether any of them know it or not.'* I chuckled.

The older female Judge began. "Our final entry of the eveni—" when the surly, now rude, bordering ignorant, Judge, leaned across the table, snatching the entry card from her hand.

Without so much as a glance at the card, he started in. "So, going to make us laugh, are you?"

'Huh? Terrific, we're back on the explanation kick again! Read the card, you twit!' After what seemed an eternity, I blurted, "God, I hope not!" His demeanor did not waver, not the least little bit. It was then I heard a very familiar laugh. Mine! Then, oddly enough, I heard a good amount of the audience laughing.

"Really? Because you sure appear funny," he flatly stated, as if to make a point. After a beat, he let out a booming laugh. Between Shirley, on my right, doing her sow impression, Jodi, off to my left, burning a hole in the side of my head with her laser stare, this demented Judge with an attitude directly in front of me, and a room full of sporadic titterers, their curiosities pushed to the edge, all I could think was, *'Another place, another time, this could be a very good thing, but just where or when, I really cannot say!'*

I could do little more than hide behind the make-up and feign a smile. *'What in hell's wrong with you? Turn the music on! Hit the damn button so I can get this over with!'*

"Does your get-up tie in with the song you're singing?"

'No, I walk around like this all the time just in case old age creeps up unannounced and I'm not paying attention! It's imperative to be ready for the inevitable!' "I'm not singing."

Finally, at long last, he looked at the registration card. "Ah, an actor!"

"Well, no."

"No?"

"Yes, no. I wrote th . . . what I'm doi . . . the story is mi . . . I'm so confused!" This bit of blather was immediately followed by the most hideous attack of nervous laughter I have ever had! The audience, most now standing, ringing the open perimeter of my space, joined in on the rather bizarre moment, apparently thinking, *'If this guy's going to have a nervous breakdown, we may as well help him along and let him go down laughing!'*

"That's okay. You've brought a story, something you've written," he concluded, sounding as if he was easing up on me.

"Yes."

"Along with music you've also written."

"No. The music isn't mine."

"Along with music you've what? Borrowed?"

'Is there a problem? 'Cause I'm about ready to walk!' I yelled, just loud enough for no one to hear. "I have the utmost respect for musicians, those who can read, write, you know, decipher the language. I've tried many times, my interpretation skills are terrible." I was trying to appeal to his sense of decency and fair play, and whatever was stuck up his butt.

"Okay." The crowd was still with me, but antsy. "But, isn't that plagiarism?"

'Fuck!' "Only at Thanksgiving!" *'What?!? Did I say what I think I just said? What?!?'* In a split second, from when that brilliant statement popped into my head, to when I opened my mouth setting it free, something odd happened. There was an abrupt silence, a pregnant pause, which lasted forever. Not only did neither the crowd nor the judge get it, even I didn't get that one! I'd lost them!

Perfectly timed, off to my left, came a friendly, somewhat silly, yet undeniably infectious, giggle. That's all it was . . . a giggle. As fast as I had lost them, one single unique sound humored the room; a simple giggle brought them back around. Jodi had single-handedly controlled the room, breaking the awkward stand-off. For the moment, I was able to stop feeling like raccoon road kill! Jodi flashed a smile. In all honesty, I didn't think I'd miss them this soon, but at that moment, those big red lips looked awfully good!

"Ladies and gentlemen, entry five, with a piece called, 'The Old Man'."

'What? Wait! That's it? No name? Where's my name? Say my name!'

And, he clicked the start button.

~~~

There's a reason, and a very good one at that, why television moguls do not schedule movies like 'It's A Wonderful Life' and 'White Christmas' during summer months. It's just not right! Unfortunately, in my zeal to scratch my new found theatre itch, the seasons of New England never came to mind. Even if they had, for creative license, it was time. This is when it had to happen.

Being a five-thumbed musician, with 'blah' vocal tones, the 'language of music' will always and forever be lost on me. I knew finding my audience as a guitar slinging Dylan was never going to happen. *'Still, there has to be a way,'* I thought, as I worked on another story. Then, nine months before, on New Years Eve, while erasing, re-writing, and re-reading, with the television on in the background, I heard 'it' and 'it' all made sense.

To mute forever this long-suffering whim of getting up in front of people, strangers, and capturing their imaginations with something *I* created, a solid, but laid back, Guy Lombardo instrumental will be my background. I found the old LP, recording the track to cassette.

For months, I suffered every single note. Writing, erasing, again and again, slaving over and over, and over still, every word, convinced, hoping, thinking, yes, praying this would work. The thinning of a line here, tweaking of a word there, opening of entire sections just for a pause, a break so, come time, anyone within earshot could/would consider the drama, the emotion being hurled at them.

Seasons of New England? Not a second of thought was spent on 'seasons'!

~~~

Two notes, that's all it took, the first two notes of my chosen background music to air for the room to recognize and react. Hearing 'Auld Lang Syne' on a leftover, hot, humid, summer-like evening in mid-September is just plain wrong!

In one ear I heard Raymond's jaw hit the floor, and Shirley snort like a pig in heat! In the other, words, my words, my voice, shaking, quaking. Straight ahead, the Judge from hell dismissed me immediately, holding a cheerful, animated gabfest with another Judge, the one who didn't want to be there to begin with, sitting two *loud* seats away!

Someone, actually a few inebriated audience members, thought the best way to express their support of entry five was exhaling with magnificent force their Tom Collins, or Vodka Collins, or what have you. The misty cascades of spritzer reminiscent of spring showers, or lawn sprinklers gone amok!

So on a sweltering late Summer's eve, with a Winter's piece of music as backdrop, what I had finished writing last Spring was about to be sprung. Fall, the only season left to plunder, was mine for the taking, and I embraced it in a face first freefall!

I tried not looking at the crowd, to not see, not hear the subdued, yet undeniable buzz of, "What the hell is this?" By staring straight ahead, all I saw, all I heard, was a windbag Judge, a motor mouth of pompous ignorance roaring in overdrive!

Now I know, compared to the woes of the world and all things important, it sounds like I'm whining over small potatoes, but, *'Goddamn it, I have something to say here!'* Maybe it may be nothing more than trite social commentary, maybe. Or, it just may be I'm poking a peephole in a topic better left in the dark, maybe, it just may be. Either way, *'Shut-up! Shut-up! Shut your mouth! Give the story half a chance!'*

Once again, I thought I was going to be sick. Why not? Par for the course to this point!

Like all manmade moments; the A-bomb drop, the assassination of the Kennedys, Tiny Tim's singing career, or the final shoulder curl leading to that first teenage orgasm, once set in motion, some things cannot be stopped!

'Is he staring at me, or am I stari . . . ? What's he star . . .' And, like in any struggle to learn, to discover, in trying, in creating, just like that, a piece of my self-made puzzle clicked and a slice of the obvious hit me; *'Eh, he can't see me! Not me! Not really, me!'*

As long as I stayed within the boundaries of this character I created, Jodi painted, I am eighty-five!

'You're my spot on the wall, Twittlehead!' I gave him a slight smile. *'Here, this is for you!'*

Our eyes fixed, locked and loaded, his with contempt, mine with a new found realization.

We were all we saw.

I ranted, raved and raged over aging, and loneliness, and forgotten souls encased in time worn shells. Over mistakes made, lives mismanaged, misery misplaced. I bore a hole in Judge's skull, there was no looking away, and he knew it! When did the crowd stop buzzing, Twittlehead cease yapping? I don't know. All I cared? That the emotion stay true to the words being spat out in eighty-five years of life. A bead of sweat, then another, broke free. The music built, my story grew, pushed to the emotional peak, the final plea, as temple veins and neck chords pulsed and swelled.

Then, as if the bottom fell out altogether, on cue, the words, the music, abruptly stopped.

Silence.

So silent, you could hear ice melt in umbrella cocktails.

I dismissed Twittlehead by closing my eyes as I told the story's end. The ease of the old man's final resolve paired musical note to written word, ending with both, fading away.

And, it was over.

'Breathe.'

I sat in limbo, in what seemed a hushed tomb. I knew I'd never be able to tell, to get across to anyone, what had happened in those three minutes. How do you explain not hearing, thinking of, or picturing a word, yet knowing every line had been delivered?

The one stage rule I knew, 'Commit to memory, then forget,' I guess I remembered well. My new rule? 'If intent on sticking your neck out, on making a spectacle of yourself, make it spectacular!' In other words, whatever you dare do, received well or not, to date, no one has pulled back a bloody stump!

Whatever works.

'Breathe.'

~~~

For months, leading up to tonight, at every private rehearsal's end, after allowing for a few seconds of ghostly applause, I would nod to the shadows. It was a simple, yet humble tilt of the head, meant to say, *'Thanks . . . thank you'*, to my fictitious audience. Finally, time allotted for the pay-off, for those many months of preparation, was at hand. The window, that moment to reap applause, nod and exit, opened and slammed shut; zip, zero, zilch, nada . . . nothing.

Without looking at anyone directly, I made a quick scan of the room. Their reaction, the look in their eyes, that is, the ones who were still looking at me, who were not shuffling a foot looking elsewhere, spoke volumes.

They got it. They got their dose of the unexpected. I gave them something to take away, just as they hoped. The problem? I'd ripped open the curtain on life too real. In my want to nail Twittlehead to the wall, I'd crucified them all, hammering my point home.

Caught in an awkward time warp, not knowing when or how to bow out gracefully, just knowing I could sit there no longer, I stood, looking down with a sheepish grin.

'Don't breathe. Don't look. Turn right and get off.'

Mid-way, on my hurried walk between here and there, someone let go a shrill whistle, followed by a positive, affirmative, "Yes!" I slowed, looked back, smiled, and gave my best nod. *'Thanks . . . thank you.'* Other audience members trickled in. Before I had chance to turn back, to square away and walk off in my intended direction, while still on the main floor, someone stepped in front of and into me. Grasping both my shoulders, I was given one firm shake. I snapped from my daze, looking up.

'It's just Raymond.'

Raymond!

His face was beet red, he seemed slightly rattled, and when he whispered, "Cool," the corners of his mouth turned down. He pulled me into him, smearing make-up on his jacket, and gave me a hug, a manly bear hug, as he pawed the back of my head. The rooms tension subsided, giving way to laughter, applause.

Our differences, our reason for the general disdain Raymond and I had for each other, was as old as time; the opposite sex. In our case; Shirley. I knew immediately why he was acting, why he was reacting the way he was and, for the moment, Shirley did not enter into it. Stepping back, I asked if he was okay. He nodded, we shook hands, he moved aside. I waded into the crowd.

The applause was not shared by all. There were a number of tissues, hankies in use.

Hurrying past, I glimpsed smiles and looks from strangers still curious, while receiving my fair share of *"atta boy'* pats on the back. But in my confused state, in wanting to gauge exactly what the material, what I had done, good or bad, at no time did I pause and take it all in, let alone stop and flat out ask.

Raymond aside, Jodi was the first of friends, of people I trusted, to make their way to me. She managed her way through a pocket of people, not hesitating in throwing her arms around me and, in a loud whisper, said, "I wish you had told me!"

I greeted her in kind, but thought, *'Wish I had told you what?'*

Dean was next with a firm handshake, shoulder slap, and bewildered look. His ruddy complexion appeared the same color as his afro. He didn't say a word. Loretta at his side, smiled.

More strangers, more looks, then I spotted the twittlehead Judge. *'I should speak to him.'* But short of apologizing, and/or asking what the hell his problem was, there was little I could think to say. I chose to walk on by.

Approaching, rounding the bar, I was showered, literally showered, with alcohol induced words of encouragement. At least I think encouragement is what they offered. I've never been good at deciphering spittle.

"Please vote," one of the Judges announced

I knew I had about fifteen minutes to get myself together and join someone; friends, a gracious stranger, anyone. For some insecure reason, I didn't want to hear the decision alone.

I stood behind the last booth, my back to everyone, changing. Between the murmur of the crowd and my racing thoughts, I didn't know what to think.

"You shouldn't have brought that here."

"What?" I turned, positive I'd heard right, but needing to hear it again to make sure.

"Why'd you bring it here? I didn't find it the least bit entertaining," said the stubby WWII doughboy. He stood there, not at all ruffled, simply voicing his cuckold opinion.

"Sorry, can't please 'em all. How do you think you did?"

Choosing to ignore my question, he repeated, "Why did you bring it here?"

"I don't know. What the hell else am I supposed to do with it? What's the problem?" He stood there, inexplicably eyeballing me.

Shirley appeared out of nowhere, practically knocking the little shit over. Lunging half over the booth, she clutched my robe, yanking me to her, and planted a kiss, a full lip lock. We ended the clench dizzy, laughing, but dizzy.

"That's why!" I chuckled, looking in his direction, but he was gone.

Funny, odd I guess, how small, near insignificant moments stick. As for the doughboy, no known explanation can be made for his attitude. The guy could sing. Isn't that enough? He has thousands (millions?) of songs to choose from and the gift, the ability, with good fortune, to deliver, to perform his heart out 'til he's six feet under. Or, maybe he'd feel better if he wrote what he sang? Or, maybe it was something else entirely. Maybe I'd hit a nerve. Maybe he was speaking for himself and any other nerves I'd pinged tonight.

'Well, excuse the fuck outta me! Present them how you wish; song, story, knock-knock joke, whatever, whichever way your creative juices flow. Erased, re-written, suffered over, one by one, over and over, 'til finally a thread is strung together just right to string a listener, a reader along. Isn't this what words are all about? To move, to humor, to make aware, to, yes, even wreak emotional havoc? If I'm wrong, if I'm missing the point to this writing thing, then I'll forever beg for my breakfast, because I'll never sing for my supper!'

As for Shirley, well, clearly she's a tart.

~~~

"Raymond's looking for you," Rick said, to his sister. She caught me looking as she walked away, flashing a smile that would give an ogre hope.

"She's killin' me, Rick! She's killin' me!" I laughed, knowing he saw our little show.

"If she doesn't, Raymond will!" he shot back, grinning.

"What'd you think?" I asked, on our walk to find a booth.

"You should get some votes."

"We'll see. But, what'd *you* think?"

"It was good."

"Good," I mimicked. "Was it *good* good? *Okay* good? *Good riddance* good?"

"How do I know? I'm a boilermaker."

"Yeah, and I'm a mailman. So?"

"So?"

"So, what'd you think?"

"It was," he started, then paused, "different."

"Different. *Different* different? *Okay* diff—"

"I don't . . ." Scowling, he slid into a booth. "I gave you my vote, how's that?"

I slid across the opposite side. "Thanks."

Breaking any sense of tension, he said, "*Thanks* thanks? *Okay* tha—"

"I tell you what; you are your sister's brother, that's for sure."

"Hey, it's a gift."

"No, I think it's more a curse!"

"Attention. Attention everyone," said the lady at the Judge's table. "We have our Adult Category winner. Emilio, if you would do the honors."

'Emilio?' Beaming, the thought, *'Emilio Twittlehead,'* entertained me

"Well, you look pleased with yourself," Jodi said, sliding in next to me. "Share?"

"Sonny."

"What?"

"Who did Sonny marry?" I grinned a silly grin.

"What?"

Continuing, "Watt. Associative light bulb term."

Finally dawning, "Uh-huh."

"Uh-uh! Too slow, I win!" I had to laugh at how quick she figured out my little game.

"I wouldn't push my luck. That could be all you win tonight."

"Point taken." But I couldn't rid myself thinking, *'Emilio Twittlehead. There's a joke in there, somewhere.'*

"In the Adult Category . . ."

"Do you feel lucky? Want the horn?" Jodi asked.

"our winner is . . ."

"I'll get it—"

"number . . ."

"after—"

"four!"

'WHAT?' "What'd he say?" I asked, trying to whisper over the room's sudden hubbub.

"Four!" The answer came from many voices, in as many different directions.

'Mister Cellophane?' "I'll be a son-of-a-bit—"

"I'm sorry! I am so sorry!" Jodi offered, in a way meant to soften the blow.

"Okay, it's okay," I said to Jodi, to the others who sat, stood, who had gathered near waiting the results. "I had to try, I had to find out."

My attempts to accept the loss in a dignified manner were almost believable, until, "I don't believe it! I don't fuc—"

"Ladies and gentlemen, if you would, please, your attention," the female Judge said, trying to snatch away the paper.

Not letting go, Emilio smiled, laughed, leaned to the microphone and, "My mistake, my mistake, chalk it up to the change of entrants order. The entry with the most votes, number five!"

My fist slammed the table top, *"Yes!"*

Hopping up on the bench seat, I stepped over Jodi, over whoever sat next to her, hitting the floor on a quick walk. My thoughts collided. On one hand I had pulled it off, while on the other . . . Looking across the room, I caught sight of Harold, Mr. Cellophane, as he faded back into the crowd. Judging from the overall clamor, most everyone expressed momentary confusion. Once I hit the open floor, the mood of the room changed, and I was met with a shower of applause, approval.

I was on a high I'd never experienced before. The best of a natural high!

Smiling, chuckling, giddy as a loon, I scurried, stopping dead center on the open floor. Facing those folks lining the right side, I looked a slow purposeful look the entire room's length, then slow back to middle, and gave a well-rehearsed nod. Spinning about, I looked left to right, one end to the other, back to center, and a nod.

I grazed upon the moment like a beggar at a banquet!

Half slide right, a nod to the bar. On to the Judges table, with a bow that'd make a bullfighter proud, and a slow, deliberate, double nod to Twittlehead. With a smooth 'shuffle-off-to-Buffalo' Jackie Gleason would approve, I made a beeline for the trophy, the ornate, garish trophy. There was but one, one, only one to be had! Confirmation!

As I bent over, as I grabbed around the base, "Whoa! Whoa! Slow down there fella!" boomed from the sound system. The demanding tone, the immediacy of command, over-powered all merriment and all merriment, went. I froze in place like a chicken feeding.

With a sideways glance, I looked to the Judge's table. *'What?'*

"That goes to New York," Emilio Twittlehead said, with a malicious grin.

Higher the high, lower the low, downer the down. *'Oh.'*

"Have first pick of one of the others. All other entrants, don't forget to pick up your trophy before you leave. Thank you all for coming. See you in New York."

Straightening up, my back to everyone, I stood looking upon a minimum of seventy trophies. Whether I took one near, one furthest away, or closed an eye and plucked one from the middle, it didn't matter. They were seventy perfectly manufactured, perfectly matched, perfectly reproduced, clones.

Seventy identical trophies!

Then, there were sixty-nine.

~5~

Doubt! Doubt! Out Damn Doubt!

With dates, contact names, and New York phone numbers in hand, I started for the door.

The night had not gone as smooth as planned, rehearsed, or dreamt. Despite not having found any clear answers as hoped, still, taken at face value, something had happened. *'Just what,'* I sniggered at the thought, *'I'm not exactly sure,'* but the piece had done something.

One thing was undeniable. I would be taking 'The Old Man' to a stage in New York City!

Leaving, the doughboy offered his congratulations. While shaking hands, with a smile on his face, he said, "Good to have friends." That was it.

My retort to the other half of this mediocre duet, "Does he really think he's all that good?" fell on deaf ears.

His quip perched atop my growing mountain of self-doubt. By telling Rick, had I subconsciously allowed him to get the word out, thus padding the count? Then there's, *'Cool.' 'Different.' 'You should have told me!'* Why hasn't one person, friend or stranger, approached me with a comment good or bad? *'Cool?'* from Raymond? Am I asking too much? *'Is anybody listening up there?'*

In the parking lot, I learned an impromptu party had been called at my place. I arrived at the Golden Rooster alone, drove home the same way. The difference? The three minutes allowed to grant my wish, find my answers, quench my want, my need to know, had evaporated. I did have a trophy though. *'Whoopie!'*

~~~

It's not as if there wasn't a party tone. I mean the air was certainly not somber, though I admit I may have been a bit in the pits. While the others raced against the late hour to pack a party in, I took a walk along the shoreline, still trying to sort the night out.

'How could the piece have won, yet still provide me with no clear anything?'

I climbed atop a pile of rocks, my self-discovered, self-proclaimed 'Boulder Isle' and sat, calmed by vast moonless ebony, stirred by breaking surf.

'Damn doughboy! Why? Why is it when you offer something different, something off the beaten path, a handful of yahoos and yokels will do their damnedest to find the slightest crack in the attempt? Staring, eyes dead, blank, they shake their heads at the unknown, shrug off the obvious, laugh the least, speak and critique in whispers, all in their need to beat you into submission. Are they intimidated? Scared? So scared their only joy is putting you back in your place? Then again, who says they have to comment? Maybe the doughboy was right. After all, what did I put it up against? A hack comic, vaudeville throwbacks, Mr. Cellophane, and a walking bodycast. No offense, but not exactly Radio City material! What was there to compare it to?

You and me, right? Were you watching? Of course you were! Did you get a kick out of this? I thought you had my back? Was I not clear enough? I figured you, if anyone, would know I was looking for more than just showing up and getting through it! More than getting up and getting the words out! Is anybody paying attention up there? Must I spell out everything?

Maybe I'm missing the point. Maybe creating is joy enough. I mean, the Mona Lisa has no eyebrows, right? How much joy was found in creating that? A lot I imagine. Is the base level of self-fulfillment found in simply doing what you do well? Is this satisfaction enough? Is that it? A master blend of colors right to the last stroke, then place it on the teetering lifetime pile? Yes? Then who will see the colors? Equal to that would have to be, from head, to finger, to keyboard, to desk drawer, wouldn't it? And, who will ever read the words? Is the hiding away of attempts, of possible gems, in a studio or writer's den, the way? Is it better to hide, afraid of exposure, safe from discussion?

Bull! The line 'tween Pornography and Art defined; If you can't masturbate to it, it's Art!

Discuss!'

~~~

"You okay? I saw you head off. Can I come up?" Jodi asked, startling me, sneaking about in the darkness.

"You wanna give me a heart attack?"

"What're you doing?" she asked, scrambling up toward me.

"Nothing, thinking."

"Of?"

"A tame and toothless tabby can't produce a lion's roar."

"Alright, I like that." She chuckled. "Did you make that up?"

"No, some dead writer."

"You keep it up, that'll be you one day."

"Thanks! What a depressing thought!"

"Well, how would you like to be remembered? Think about it. Everybody dies. We all tire and die. The difference is, well, trying. So would you rather be some tired guy who never tried and died? Or, an artist, a sculptor, a writer, who died tired trying?" There was a brief pause, then she chuckled. "Try that three times fast!"

"That sorta makes sense . . . no, no it doesn't."

"Does too! Alright, could've been better, but go with the gist. It's there."

"I get the gist."

"That's it? Wow, tough crowd. There was a double gist in there and . . . never mind. So, when's New York?"

"November seven—"

"Great! So?"

"Eighth, ninth, and tenth. So? So, what?"

"Four days? So, are we going?"

"I am."

"Well, that was about as subtle as a lobotomy!"

"What? So far, no one, not even you, has said a thing. 'I wish you had told me' tells me nothing!"

Standing, she said, "Yeah, you're right. You have time to find someone else. Good luck!"

"Are you mad?"

"Know what your problem is? You've really got to get over yourself!"

"Hey, fact is—"

"Facts my ass! Okay, fact, we're even! You wrote it; you made it up. Then, fact, I made you up with a stellar make-up job! I know you want to think you did this all by your little ol' self, but, fact is, when you won, I won! By the way, where's my trophy? You didn't get me one did you? That's okay, I'll take yours!"

"Is that a fact?"

"You catch on quick! Oh, I was wrong. Pay-up the twenty-five dollars we agreed to, not for services, for cost, then we'll be even! Shove New York!"

"I figured you wouldn't want to go. If you can't get into what this is all about, why would you want to? Honestly, the more I thought about it, the more I figured you were, I don't know, embarrassed or, I don't know . . . something like that!"

"I can't get into what it's all about?" she mocked, somewhat flabbergasted. "You wrote it and you can't even define it! You don't even know what it is you wrote; let alone what to call it! What was it Rick said? Different? It's 'different'? You were looking for a way out of here, maybe get on a New York stage. Well, being 'different' is what's going to get you there! You just may have to be happy with that! Every time you do this—"

"Sh."

" . . . a lot of people are going to wonder, 'Why?'"

"Sh-h."

"But, more will say, 'Why not?' Did you just shush me?"

"Boy, when you get on a roll!"

"What?"

"Will you go to New York with us?"

"Us?"

"Me and my 'different' old friend?"

"No."

"No?"

"Not unless we agree to a few things."

"Is this going to take long?"

"First, you don't ask my opinion again," she began, sitting back down. "I will not get caught up in your battle to sort this out. Second, how good a show this organization is going to present, we'll have to wait and see. But, it's at the Biltmore, how bad can it be? Be professional, you never know who's watching. How many is that?"

"Two. Are there many more?"

"My name's not really Jodi, it's Dawn."

"You're a transvestite?"

"Not D-O-N!" She laughed, heartily. "D-A-W-N! Are you bipolar?"

"No! Straight! Why?"

"I can't tell when you're serious or not. So which one's it going to be?"

"Which one what?"

"Jodi or Dawn?"

"You're confusing and a little weird yourself, you know that, right? I think I'll stay with Jodi, strictly for 'professional' reasons."

"Good choice."

"Why don't you like Dawn? I think it's a nice name."

"Brings back bad memories. An old boyfriend's one joke . . . never mind."

"What?"

"Was telling his buddies he liked waking up at the crack of Dawn!"

"No sir! You lie! That's funny!" Daggers shot from her squinting eyes. "No it isn't!" I recanted, swallowing back a laugh. She stared, knowing I'd crack. I did! "I'm sorry, but it is funny!"

"Yeah, the first time! It's late, I should be going."

"Why? You're welcome to stay."

"Oh, smooth! Not tonight. Tonight, I'm a good girl. Good girls go to heaven, you know."

"Yeah, but bad girls go every—"

"Well, this one will get to New York anyway! It's late. I have two full productions to make-up tomor . . . Today! Tonight! Do you have my money?"

"Sure." I leaned right, digging for my back pocket wallet. "If you're strapped, I can loan you a few bucks."

She leaned left, positioning her hand on the mist damp boulder. "Who said anything about being strapped?" She pushed up, saying, "This is business," and her hand slipped. Our heads rapped hard, so hard we clearly heard the hollow 'clunk' followed by 'echo, echo, echo' as lightning bolts and multi-colored shooting stars flash-danced brighter than any marquee on Broadway!

Falling into each other for involuntary support and leverage, polite exchanges of, "Ow! Are you okay?" never came. We opted instead for immediate direct relief through maniacal moaning and wounded wailing. Gales of giggly groans were thrown into the mix, shaken, not stirred. We made noises best described as sounding like a pair of horny hyenas in heat! We carried on, oblivious to the likely skull fracture, possible concussion, certain contusions, and the absolute certainty of two, soon to be hideous, black and blue goose eggs!

Confused tears of pain and laughter flowed, nose and mouth bubbles formed and burst, each of us racing to be the first to fashion a coherent word!

"R u o k?" was as close as I could come to babbling anything even near intelligent.

Jodi responded just enough to let me know she wasn't knocked senseless, without control of her motor skills, or dead. Sticking her thumb up, she said, "I b a-ok. U?"

"I b too," I replied, impressed, given the circumstances, at any conversational abilities.

"I go," she said, struggling to lift her heavy head from my neck and shoulder.

"Me go too."

"U a me go?"

"Si," was all I said, and she lost it! Now, I'm no authority on matters of heart or humor, and I'll be the first to admit to heights of silliness, but the girl absolutely exploded, plunging into a fit of convulsive laughter! Her head slid off my shoulder and dropped, just fell, her forehead crashing into my crotch, her left shoulder crunching my kidneys!

My head pain momentarily vanished, having been displaced, desperately dispatched, to a new found area of screaming discomfort!

As much as I felt a need to soothe something on me, to be honest, the rhythmic laughing, the pulsing massage of her shoulder and forehead, felt nice, odd, but nice, certainly far better than I could do for myself at the moment!

Her forehead and shoulder buried, I set my right hand on her head and, gently patting, said, "There, there." She collapsed! Though fully clothed, I felt her entire form turn to a quivering, albeit soothing, sac of human Jell-O!

This is when the thought occurred to me, *'What a wonderful laugh! We're clicking! I'm having a oft heard 'fate-filled moment' over a laugh! No! We're having a oft heard fate-filled moment over a laugh! Well, I'm having a oft heard fate-filled moment, she's doing all she can to breathe!'* "Do you smoke?" I asked, suddenly concerned.

"No," she managed to squeal.

"Excellent! You'll be fine! Relax." I waited 'til she was somewhat composed, then, "I spent a year up in Maine—"

"Oh?" she muttered.

" . . . one week." And again, she went right over the edge! *'What a beautiful noise!'* As I told my tale, I pondered what little I knew of her, running through her vital stats.

Age? *'Perfect!'*

"Spent many a vacation visitin' with ol' Gran'pap—"

"Ah."

" . . . a-yuh, up in East Bumphuck, Maine!" Helpless, hopeless, she tried with no luck regaining composure. "Christmas Eve, nineteen-hunnert-fiffy-eight. I was seven. A blizzard hit, immobilizin' East Bumphuck, strandin' me and my family at Gran'paps."

Height? *'Perfect!'*

"No!"

"A-yuh!"

"No more!"

"Sad his four gran'chillen would wake to empty Christmas stockin's, Gran'pap stepped out inna that blizzard, goin' a-shoppin'!"

Weight? *'Perfect!'*

"Stop," I think she said. "Please!" she wheezed. I felt the motion of her right hand slide up my right pant's leg.

"Christmas morn, we gran'chillen each found lucky rabbit foots in our stockin's. Mom, a furry hand muff. Dad, a pair of warm, fuzzy, earmuffs. And, for Christmas dinner we gave thanks, feasting on bowls of Gran'pap's own secret recipe, 'Rabbit Stew a la Gran'pap!'"

Love of stage? *'Perfect!'*

"No more!" she rasped, her hand now gracing my upper inner thigh.

"It was a perfect Polaroid pictorial; 'Christmas in East Bumphuck—'"

"Stop!"

'. . . fiffy-eight!'

Boyfriend/Husband? *'No!'*

"Please—"

"Well, it would've been perfect—"

"STOP!"

" . . . if Hoppy hadn't disappeared!" The poor girl went limp. *'YAHTZEE!'* Absolutely collapsed!

"YEEEOWWWW!" I yelped as, in an attempt to shut me up, she grabbed and squeezed a handful of fleshy inner thigh!

Jodi lay there motionless, speechless. *'Did she stop breathing?'* I'd heard stories of people laughing themselves to death, but never thought it possible.

I grasped her shoulders, trying to help. She rose from my crot . . ."Ow!" . . . lap, slowly. The grip she held on my inner thigh felt, I'm sure, just like a horse bite would!

Hoots and hollers were heard from revelers leaving the party, panning headlights swept across the open span of shoreline. What seconds ago was near total darkness, now was filled with shadow-dancing silhouettes, flitting in and out, around and about Boulder Isle.

The more Jodi rose, the more she calmed, regaining some sense of composure. She awarded me for every inch gained, and for keeping quiet, by easing her grip. " . . . ouch . . ."

'Either one enormous nose bubble just burst, or she licked me, 'cause suddenly I'm feeling moist about the Adam's apple!' In seconds, her sweaty cheek would be level to my chin. *'I haven't had a total meltdown like this since, since, in memory!'* I consciously embraced the idea of her turning to me. Time, a lot of time, had slipped away since I last felt even remotely close to finding the missing puzzle piece, to filling the gaping hole in my jig-saw heart.

'Whoa! Pull back, Pearl Buck! What if she didn't feel it? Huh? What if the moment went right over her head? Or, what if she did feel it, liked it, but chooses not to act on it? Worse, what if she did feel it, but didn't like it? What then?'

Doubt! Doubt! Out damn doubt!

'Of course she felt it! She must have felt it! I felt it! And, why wouldn't she like it? She had to like it! I liked it! And I haven't felt anything I liked like it in a long, long, time!'

A decision must be made! *'Decisions, decisions, deci . . .* 'Now!

'If she wanted wanting, needed needing, knew anything about caring and being cared for, these alone . . . What a terrific trifecta! But, maybe, just maybe, if she could love, be loved, share love, as long, as hard, as true, as she could laugh, and near daily, as an extra added bonus, show me, teach me how, I will right now, after a lifetime of disbelief, recant,

and atop the highest peak, on a stack of Bibles, swear to a caring, giving, merciful God!'

Maybe.

I made up my mind; I may have shied away back at the restaurant, but a second opportunity would not be missed, another chance would not be allowed to fall away!

Back at the house, backfires and guttural rumblings from Dean's heavy duty pick-up truck kicking over, caused me to straighten up. Headlights flicked on, casting the night around Boulder Isle into a veiled shade of gray. The mist on the back of Jodi's head shone. Rather, her soft, tousled, misty ash blonde hair sparkled, off the same light I squinted into.

What happened next happened pretty quick. Jodi's head began to turn. Dean's truck stalled. The headlights went out.

Her face so near, our mouths so close. *'Is that cherry Chap-Stick?'* My senses twitched.

Just as Jodi and I were about to make *'contact'*, Dean's pick-up roared back to life and he flipped a switch. Dual, heavy duty, high-powered, roof mounted search lights lit up Boulder Isle like a mid-summer's day, illuminating the, now smeared, colors on Jodi's face!

To simply say I flinched is like saying the Boston Strangler was simply misunderstood!

With eyes wide to the point of popping, my mouth fell open and, in a desperate attempt to escape, through clamped tight vocal chords, a primal noise strangled, dying in my throat! I actually felt myself, in ultra slow motion, recoil! Struggling to inhale, air finally rushed in, only to crash head-on with yet another form of self-expression rushing to get out! The only sounds heard were five air tight bursts and a stretched taut, single flat note. A noise best categorized as a shriek!

I shrieked! That's right, shrieked!

At the same singular moment my shriek squeezed out, thought and word conspired to be one. For lack of a better explanation, I was overwhelmed with desire, nay, need to speak, explain my behavior. And I did so, blurting, "The make-up has got to go!"

Better to have shrieked . . . again!

Unable to see her face past the make-up, the look she gave me was, at best, indescribable!

Her eyes told her feelings. Her eyes spoke volumes. I caught her look just as Dean's searchlights went out, just as she shoved me back, pushed me away. If the eyes are windows to the soul, what I witnessed was shock, pain, hurt and humiliation. Along with those, what I felt, what I was left feeling when she slammed the window of opportunity shut, were rude, ignorant, stupid, and a few other choice adjectives one can only call themselves!

My sputtered attempts at explanation, "Jodi!" my rushed ramblings of apology, "Stop!" fell on deaf ears. "I'm sorry!" To make matters worse, "Say something!" she would not say a word. Sounds came from her as she squared away and stood, but nothing near remotely intelligible. "I wish I could take it back!"

Hearing her attempt to scurry down from the boulders in the shadows, I stood, extending my hand in her general direction. The sound of her mis-steps, her shoes slipping, sliding off the rocks, warned of the inevitable.

"I was . . . I didn't mean . . . you caught me off . . . please! I have this thing about clowns!"

"Now I'm a . . . (slip, bang, thump) . . . oof . . . clown?" she whimpered, now physically, as well as emotionally, shaken.

Following the sound of her choked back sobs, I found her at the base of the boulders sitting on the sand, a little banged up, but none the worse for wear. "Are you okay?"

"Go to hell!"

"You're mad," I offered.

"Will you stop saying that! I may be upset, stubborn, unreasonable, even slightly off my rocker, but I am not *mad!*"

"A little angry, perhaps?" Clearly, I heard her snort back a laugh through a whimper. "I just want to say—"

"What? What do you want to say?" she asked, in a edgy, tricky tone.

"Well, for starters, that was very unladylike. Are you going to be making noises like that when we're in New York?" I saw a grin as her silhouette turned in my direction.

Now humored, she laughed. I sighed in relief. Then, "It's not going to work," she said.

"Who are you to say? Just cut back on the make . . ." I knew when I said it, it was too soon.

"Who are you to tell me, 'cut back on the make-up'? What . . . who are you? It's what I do!"

"I know, and you do it very well, but that doesn't mean it appeals to everyone. I mean, not everyone likes everything I write."

"Maybe you're a sucky writer! Ever stop and consider that?"

"I didn't mean *everyone!*" After a lull, "Well," I sighed, "we could camp out here for the night."

"I really have to go."

I helped her stand. "Come on, I'll walk you to your car." But for the sound of waves breaking, we walked along in silence. Stepping from the shadows of the moonless beach, into the dim light of nearby streetlamps, I asked, "Are we okay?"

"I'm fine."

"Not you, we?"

Thinking, hesitating, she finally said, "We're fine, okay, I guess."
I heard a smile in her voice. Looking at her, my eyes fell right to
the alien looking goose egg on her forehead which, with the colors
mooshed all over, made it appear like a tiny mutating head. I looked
away, fast. "Who's Shirley?"

"What? Rick's sister. Raymond's girlfriend. Why?"

Ignoring my question, she moved right along. "Do you all share each
other's girlfriends so casually?"

"I . . . I'm not . . . what?"

"I saw you kissing."

"Oh."

"A couple of times."

"Oh, that. I don't even like the guy."

"Not him!" She laughed aloud. "I saw you kissing her."

"See, it could have been a lot worse! *'What a great laugh!'* It was just
a peck."

"I'm not familiar with the 'peck'. It looked a lot like the French kiss."

"Yeah, they do have similarities," I said, trying to joke it off. "We
dated one time. We're friends. A good luck peck. Like the horn you
gave me, but with better aftertaste."

"What's with the clown phobia?"

As much as I wanted, I couldn't look her way. "I don't know. I think
it's from watching old circus movies," I told her, staring at my feet
as we walked. "Have you ever seen one where the clown wasn't the
bad guy, let alone the psycho murderer? Then at the end, when
they're taking him away, the make-up's either half off, or smeared
all over his face. And the nose, the bulbous red nose, ends up totally
bent out of shape or missing completely! Don't get me started on

midget clowns! Fifty li'l killers crammed in a VW bug! I'll be up all night!"

She laughed like I remembered, then stopped walking. "This is good." I stopped and she, in very brisk steps, scooted ahead of me. "I parked around the other side of the house. I can make it from here."

"I don't mind," I said, taking a step forward.

"No! I'll call you over the weekend. Bye." She ran off, without looking back. I stood watching until she disappeared around the house.

Walking towards the driveway, past overgrown bushes, I couldn't help but think about all that just happened. *'As bad as it could have ended . . . '* I had to chuckle, even laugh out loud, thinking about moments, about Jodi. Her laugh. Her humor. Her interests. My interests. Our interests.

'The make-up has got to go! I don't believe I said that!' Honesty is a multi-thorned prick.

At the same time I saw a set of headlights appear from the other side of the house, I heard a rustle in the bushes, and stopped. Rick waved as he drove past. Raymond stepped out from the bushes. "The bathroom works, you know," I said, as he got in his car. "Forgetting something?"

"I shook twice."

"Shirley?"

"She went home with Rick," he said, starting the car. "Gotta run." And he drove off.

With everyone now gone, I made my way to the steps leading to the kitchen door, wondering how my impromptu party went over. As I was about to step in, I heard 'putt-putt-putt' and another set of headlights came from around the side of the house. I strained to see who and what as it passed under the streetlamp. It was Jodi. In a

VW bug! A clown car, but not just any clown car, this was orange! Beeping, waving; I chuckled then shuddered, knowing I'd be awake all night!

Entering the kitchen, the mess I found, almost made me glad . . . almost. *'Well, I won't be sleeping; at least I have something to keep me busy.'* I kicked aside a few beer cans making my way to the living room. I flicked on the lights. "Brothers are a wonderful thing, aren't they?" Reacting, I ducked!

"I wouldn't know," I said, still crouched, not believing my eyes. "Raymond said you went home with Rick."

"As I said, aren't brothers a wonder—"

"I . . . I'm not sure," I stammered. "Did you two have an argument? Do you need a ride?"

"No, we didn't, and yes, I do; after breakfast. Why? Is that okay?"

"Why not? Sure," I said, unsure. "But, why?" I asked, hoping she'd draw me a map.

"Why?" she quizzed, scowling. "I don't know. I think maybe I have this thing for old men." We laughed. "Why do you think?"

"What about Raymond?" I cautiously asked, finally comfortable to stand straight.

"I have an idea . . . let's not tell him. Won't he be in for a treat in his old age?" She winked, her baby blues sparkled. "This is a cute place," she said, getting up from the easy chair.

"Thanks. That's the kitchen. This is what's left of the living room."

"Yeah, I know, I've seen it. What's up the stairs?"

"The bedroom."

"I haven't seen that." She smiled, every pearly white in her head glistening.

"Would you like to?"

"Would I?" she exclaimed, with comical excitement, firmly placing a foot on the first step.

"Hare lip! Hare lip!"

She stopped. "What? What'd you say?" her once flirty tone now flat.

"It's an old joke!" The silence was not conducive to the merriment at hand. "Friends try convincing another friend, who happened to have a wooden eye, to go to the dance. Still not comfortable, he agrees anyway. Now at the dance, they talk him into asking Mary, a nice girl, but with a hare lip, to dance. She gets so excited when he asks her, she shouts, "Would I? Would I?" Thinking she's poking fun at him, he shouts, "Hare lip! Hare lip!" Shirley just stared at me. "I said it was old. Not funny."

"Do you have any more?"

"No, I think that's it."

"Good!" I got the message.

I reached around, flipping off the kitchen light. Shirley continued up the stairs. I turned off the last house light in the living room, and started up right behind her. Mere minutes into entering 'Featherbed Lane', we heard a motor idling, seconds later, a rap on the door.

"It's Raymond!" she whispered, wide-eyed.

"Don't say that!"

"It's not Raymond!" she snorted.

"Then who is it?"

"It's Raymond!" Her piggish laugh tore through the room.

"I'm going to check."

"Don't turn any lights on."

"I won't," I said, standing at the top of the stairs.

"Here, take this for good luck." She snapped her bra in my direction. I heard it land down the stairs.

"I've been given an Italian horn, a French peck, and now a Victoria's Secret bra. How much luck can one guy have?" I laughed aloud. From the silence, and lack of shadow movement, I knew Shirley just stared at me. "Never mind. Don't go away."

I felt my way through the darkness, down the stairs, stepped on the bra's hooks, "Ow!" kicked it into the kitchen, and made my way to the backdoor. All the while I couldn't stop thinking, *Jodi would've thought that funny, and laughed at my tasteless joke, too. Boy, that's a large bra! What am I doing?'*

I peered out the window, opened the door. An envelope with scribbled writing was stuck in the outer door handle. I stepped out, took the envelope, crossed the front yard, and stood under the foggy street lamp. *'Three strikes and you're out!'* I read. *'Careful, you already have two. You did great tonight. New York, watch out! Don't ask again! Sleep tight. Don't let the bed, oh, you don't like bugs. I forgot to give you this. It may help keep you out of trouble. I have to be in the area tomorrow. Maybe I'll stop in. Talk soon.'*

Looking down the road, I watched the faint red taillights of Jodi's VW disappear.

Looking up to the bedroom, the flame from Shirley's cigarette lighter lit up the windows, then went dark.

Looking at the Italian horn, I knew another decision was at hand.

'Decisions, decisions, decisions!'

~6~

Tics 'n Flits

I awoke, tucked away in a dry, cozy, Boulder Isle crevice, still clutching Jodi's 'good luck' gift, the chain wrapped around my fingers. Comfortable, I lay there, entertained by nature's perks; rays of morning sun, playful noise of sandpipers, lazy lapping of minor waves barely reaching, lightly breaking, the shore.

At the very least I was convinced Shirley now thought me a rude host and lost cause. *'Oh, hell, damage done.'* So, I walked the beach, thinking about last night's show, of New York, of Jodi. *'Jodi.'* I caught myself grinning.

'First things first,' I thought, as I quietly opened the kitchen door, making my way up the bedroom stairs. Much to my surprise, shock, and unthinkable wish, Shirley lay there in her rubenesque splendor, bare, plain and simple, sleeping on her right side, her back to me. I spun around to head back downstairs and stopped. *'Could I?'*

Needing a moment to think, aware of possible trauma waking up in strange surroundings may cause her, I took a seat in the corner chair. Taking up my latest copy of Field 'n Stream, opening to 'Migration of the Large Mouth Bass', I began to read, with no such luck. *'Should I?'*

My visible inventory listed her neck as kissable, shoulders lickable, back pliable. The slope of her waist, rise and fall of her bubble butt, down ivory thighs, over creamy calves, to small ankles, little feet. *'Would I? Hare lip! Hare lip!'*

I worked my way back up again, and down, and up, and . . . all the while wishing I had moved the full-length mirror to the other side of the bedroom!

After what seemed, no, what was, hours of on again off again dozing by me, of waiting and, to be honest, fantasizing, Shirley finally stirred. Turning, she grabbed the sheet up around her. Moving to the bed, I smiled, joking, "Was it good for you?" I spied nippleage.

"Don't be funny!" she snapped in ill humor. "What time is it? What happened to you?"

"Ten, ten-thirty. I dozed off on the beach. The sun woke—"

"Speaking of . . . why don't you put some curtains up to block the damn sun out?" She grabbed her blouse. "Listen to those annoying gulls!" Got up. "That monotonous splashing!" Found her pants. "How do you stand it?" And proceeded to dress.

"Perils of renting," I agreed, appeasing her, but grimacing at the irony.

"Well, I hope you have better luck next time!"

"You and me both." Up to this point, even with her sour attitude and discovery of her piggish laugh, if the gods of 'Sex for Sex Sake' were to intervene with a 'quick' blessing, I might have overlooked her brittle tone. But, right about here, the China-doll image I had created, a facade Shirley supported, began cracking wide open. First the obvious; *'Damn she's testy!'*

"What?" *'And deaf!'* "Where's my bra?" *'With humongous, dangerous breasts!'* "You didn't think we were going to, now, did you?" *'And controlling!'* "You had your chance, buddy!" *'And vain!'*

"How about a rain check?"

"How about my bra?" *'And an Indian-giver!'*

"Oh, you want it back?" I smiled, not knowing when to quit. "I thought you gave it to me as a good luck piece."

"That's just what you need, too. A good piece!" I had to smile. "Of luck!" *'And smarmy!'*

"So, I can keep it then?" I joked, somehow knowing I had carried this one bit too far.

She knelt one knee on the bed, put her hands flat for support, leaned in to me, and in a most clear, concise, succinct tone, and dead-on word choice said, "Find my fucking bra!" Though her exposed mammoth mammary glands dangled under my chin, because of her state, I dared not sneak a peek. Shirley was rapidly losing her premier standing with me.

"It flew downstairs when you snapped it at me!" I exclaimed, as she shoved, pushing me over the side of the bed. "Stop pulling the bed apart!"

Something told me she didn't care for the way I spoke to her. I think it was how she stared at me, all bug-eyed, is what gave her away. This, and her unnerving sudden silence, sucking all life out of the room like a fire blanket! Finally, "Well, fly down and get it!" she commanded.

Now, normally I would have stood firm of ground, even to the point of being a bonehead in not being pushed around. However, I don't know, maybe it's just me, but there's something about a red-faced, white knuckled, eye-popping woman, nipples fully erect without the frenzy of foreplay, which will cause any life loving male to reassess his priorities! I wasted no time going downstairs.

"Coffee," she said, more telling than requesting.

"Yeah." *'Damn!'* "I'm out of filters."

"You're an actor! Improvise!"

'I'll strain it through your triple D's if you don't stop being so damn bossy!'

"Hi."

"Geezus!" I yelped, spinning around. Looking at who spoke, knowing I should know her, knowing I did, but not quick to recognize, I whimpered, "Geez . . ." a second time.

"Stop being an ass and throw it up here!" bellowed clueless Princess Shirley

'Who the . . . ?' She handed me the bra, I tossed it up the stairs. The Grand Teton's boulder holder landed short of the top step. "Little more wrist there, Priscilla!" Shirley chided.

"She's funny," said my unexpected guest, giggling.

"Sh, no she's . . ." I started to say. I motioned her away from the living room entrance, over to the kitchen's backdoor. I know I bordered rude staring, and I know it sounds a schmaltzy 'pulp novel' thing to say, but I found myself looking into the face of everything I ever dreamt of, ever wanted. Funny, though I could never, for any amount of money, explain perfection, perfection defined stood before me. "Jodi?" She smiled a faint, shy smile. "What'd you do?" I asked, starting a whispered conversation.

"The door was open. I shouldn't have, I should leave."

"No. I mean, your face! What'd you do to your . . . I mean—"

"Nothing. No, that's not . . . about last night. I thought I'd stop by to show . . . to say . . ." she stumbled. Taking a breath, trying again, "How's your foreski . . . head! Forehead! Bump? Forget I said . . . your impression's wrong. Was. Maybe."

"Oh?"

"Yes."

"That's easy for you to say," I quipped, she laughed. "You look terrific!" And she did. She was, but for a touch, completely free of any applied color. With the make-up gone I saw a natural blushing tone, a dimple in her right cheek, but it wasn't all about looks. Now, in the light of day, I saw a swimmer's build, and further, I suddenly realized she stood a mere four inches shorter than my six-one. I could not help but stare. Not in a lewd, lustful way, but in the same dumbfounded way prospectors get when they find a long searched for nugget of gold, or the look a moose gets when caught in the headlights.

At that precise moment, the thought of last night, of her and I on Boulder Isle, of being wrong, of doubting, chalking up to fiction those age-old stories of someone for everyone, hit me. I now knew those old lines I'd heard, of everyone having someone walking around looking to connect, were actually true. Living proof stood before me, in my very own kitchen!

"What the hell you doing? Picking the beans?" Countess Shirley bellowed.

"Your girlfriend's calling you," Jodi whispered, through a grin.

"I've a few things I'd like to call her, 'girlfriend' is not one, believe me!" She laughed. "Sh, I hope you don't think anything . . . I mean, I know this looks like something . . . but believe me nothing—"

"I've been here long enough, waiting for you to come down. I heard everything."

"Everything?"

"Nothing. Would you like to join me for breakfast? I mean after you give her some coffee?"

"I'm all out of filters," I started to explain, when she took a cup from the dish strainer, pouring the remainder of her donut shoppe coffee in.

"Cream, no sugar, sir," she said, in a clerk's cheery tone.

I had to laugh. "Perfect. Thank you."

"Cream, no sugar?" I yelled to the Duchess.

"Black! Three sugars!" We burst out laughing, making sourpuss looks at the thought.

"I think she needs all the sweetening she can get," I whispered. Jodi giggled, watching as I shoveled three heaping teaspoons in. "I'll take this to her, then we'll grab some breakfa—"

"Who're you talking to?" hollered Princess Eagle Ears.

"Damn, I have to take her home!" I whispered.

"Maybe not," Jodi said, looking out the door.

"No, I told her I would."

"Shirley?" snarled an angry Raymond, standing in the driveway.

"I think Raymond lost something," Jodi said, with a humored scowl.

"Raymond?" I went to the door. "What the hell's he doing here?"

"Raymond?" Shirley yelled.

"Get out here!" Raymond demanded.

"Who does he want? Shirley or me?"

"Let's hope it's not you," Jodi said through a chuckle. "I've seen his type before."

"What type is that?"

"Big!" She covered her mouth, trying not to laugh at herself. "Does this happen to you often?"

"No!" I exclaimed, as Raymond and Shirley held one of the most heart rendering dialogues of the twentieth century.

"Shirley!" said Raymond.

"Raymond!" said Shirley.

"Douche bag!" said Raymond.

"Asshole!" said Shirley.

"Whore!" said Raymond.

"Shit for brains!" said Shirley.

Conceding a draw, Raymond eyed the door, turning his attention to me. "Her mother's not as big a liar as her brother! You think you're some sorta Casa-friggen-nova? Get your ass out here! Now!"

"I think he'd like to speak to you," Jodi said. I couldn't help but laugh at her nonchalant manner, her mellow demeanor; still, something told me she was concerned.

I opened the door. "You talking to me, Raymond?"

"That's it," Jodi tittered, "keep him off guard." Patting my back, she ducked behind me.

"Well, he ain't talkin' to me!" Shirley offered, disqualifying herself.

"You did my woman, didn't you?"

"No, Raymond, I did not *do* your woman."

"Yes you did, you lying sack of sh—"

"He didn't do diddly!"

"Can't find one of your own so you got to steal mine? I'm gonna rip your frigg—"

Jodi came out from hiding. "Hi, Raymond."

"Who's that?" Raymond asked, totally blindsided

"Raymond, Jodi. Jodi, Raymond."

"Who?" asked Shirley.

"What're you . . . a friggen owl?"

"Bite me, Raymond!"

"Jodi, Shirley. Shirley, Jodi."

"Hi."

"Hi."

"What the . . ." Raymond stuttered. "What're you . . . doin' two women in there?"

"Raymond, I'm not *doin'* either of them!"

"Can't act, and can't fu—"

"Raymond, you are such a Neanderthal!" Shirley offered in my defense . . . I think.

"Let's go!"

Overhead, Shirley stomped across the bedroom floor as I tried, one last time, to make Raymond understand. "Raymond . . ." Down the stairs Shirley bounced. "think what you will . . ." Entered the kitchen, "but just for the record . . ." pushed me aside, "I'm telling you . . ." greeted Jodi and, "I never touched her!" bra in hand, "Bye!" out the door she went.

"The hooks are all bent," was all she said to me.

"Go to hell, fagg . . ." Raymond started, stopping short at Shirley's appearance.

Shirley swung her bra at Raymond, "Say one more word . . ." climbed in the passenger side, "and I tell everyone . . ." and slammed the door. "about your three testicles!" Raymond glared at me.

"What'd she say?" Jodi asked.

"Something about three testicles."

"We didn't hear that!" Jodi yelled, slamming shut the kitchen door. We crouched at the window peeking out, as Raymond got behind the wheel. We collapsed at the sight of Shirley, flailing away at Raymond with her bra, as the animated lovers drove off.

"She'll kill him!" I chuckled, opening the door, watching them disappear down the road.

"If she were in it, definitely!" Jodi's easy manner, "Something tells me he likes it though." and infectious laughter, "He'll survive." I found both refreshing and welcome.

"So, breakfast? We could go out, but I think I can whip up breakfast for two."

"Oh, you cook?" she asked, as I foraged inside the refrigerator.

"Are you kidding? I can do things with an egg that'd make a chicken blush!"

I glanced at her. First, because I enjoyed looking at her, second, because no girl, no woman, no female ever made me feel this at ease, this comfortable. And third, despite all signals sent from head, to heart, to inseam, reading, 'Positive! All Systems Go!' being the insecure bumbler I am at times with the ladies, I sought reassurance she at least thought me witty. Glancing, I saw from her reaction to my egg reference, she did.

Standing in the open doorway facing me, the morning sun sparkled, washing over, and in some areas through, her ash brown hair, white shorts, her thin white blouse. Sunbeams danced, bouncing off her arms and legs. The way the rays bathed her, highlighting her face, her smile, her figure, I had to grin, thinking, *'This is as close as I'll ever be to seeing a vision . . . Biblical or not!'*

The words, *'I want you more than life itself!'* screamed to be heard, but what came out was, "How would you like your eggs?" *'Upstairs?'* "Omelet?" *'Horizontal?'* "Scrambled?" *'Between the sheets?'* "Hard?" *'Naked!'* "Over easy?" *'Now!'*

With a coy look, she said, "I know what you're thinking."

I felt my face redden. "Believe me, you have no idea."

"Oh? Okay. Ask me a question."

"Would you prefer panca—"

"Not to do with food."

'Careful,' I thought, though convinced, *'it's not just me.'* "I hope, that is, I think I know the answer to this, but—"

"Yes?"

"Are you seeing anyone?"

"Yes." I was stunned, frozen. "You." Relieved, quick to thaw, I caught myself tilting, tipping in to her. She half-stepped in, I moved forward. My hands went to her waist. She moved in, I half-stepped the rest. Her arms draped my shoulders. "And you?" she whispered.

"Me too." I caught my breath. "You." Nanoseconds before consummating our first kiss, I heard the slightest 'tic', the smallest sound of an oral 'tic', nanoseconds later, I'd forgotten it. The kiss wasn't the only pleasure found. I had to smile when, much to my delight, I found myself standing fully erect, not all hunched and bent, bending to meet the moment. Having to conform, contort to accommodate another's height, can at times be quite awkward, as I've found too many times over the years. For example, it really is quite humiliating when a six foot one inch frame makes the first move on a five foot two inch frame, only to be rebuffed!

Needless to say, but wanting to be clear, I was in height heaven!

Whether time stopped or rushed on by, either way, I lost track, struck with the thought, *'She may need air.'* Not wanting to stop, but not wanting to appear a total lip glutton, I let my pucker pale. Our mouths parted ever so slight. I heard a faint gurgle as she inhaled, felt the moisture of her exhale.

'tic'

I wanted, needed, had to go back for seconds. Jodi shared my hunger. *'What a nice thing.'*

She wrapped her arms around my neck. I ushered her in from the small of her back. Heads moved, arms pulled, tongues met, sliding, gliding, darting, under, over, under and over, under and . . . *'Oh, where the hell have you been?'* I knew when this clench ended one of us would be left standing alone, as the other would've been consumed, totally absorbed!

Eyes shut, the sounds of oral swordplay swished in rhythm, as teeth nicked in time with most every thrust. Needy, greedy, hungry hearts fed off conscience free souls, as we imitated immovable mountains, neither willing to give an inch. She was the rock to my hard place.

Mouths twitched, eyelids shuttered, the purple haze lifted. Rational thinking crept in as soft, smooth tongues, sadly retreated. What just moments earlier flew open, was now slow to close. Moist lips lingered, set upon same, as we casually caressed the end of the first kiss, the beginning of many.

'tic'

With a shy look, Jodi whispered, "Thank you."

'For making the earth move?' I smiled. "For what?"

"Dislodging that hairball."

'tic'

Somewhat dizzy, and a little weak kneed, her reply proved our undoing. Still holding on, though limp and loose, we erupted in laughter and began to teeter off kilter. Swaying, with the feeling of imminent collapse, Jodi wrapped her left leg about my right. We stood like a deformed flamingo, balanced, one being with three legs, but in control.

"Please don't think I'm, well, being—" I started to say.

"Yes?"

"Would you like to go upstairs?"

"No."

"I understand."

"I'd rather stay down here with you." 'tic'

"That's old, funny, but old. What is that?"

"What?"

"You're making a tic."

"I am? I thought it was you." She smiled. 'tic' "What's that?"

"The tic."

"Not that."

"What?"

"That! Your eyebrow is spazzing."

"It is not . . . it is, isn't it?" And it was. I wouldn't call the twitch a spasm, but sure enough, my left eyebrow flitted away, not of my doing. Looking down, it stopped. Looking at her, it started. Looking away, it calmed. Looking back, again it began. "Hmph, I'll be damned!"

"What?"

"Don't you see what we're doing?" I playfully pleaded.

"What?"

"We're infecting each other with tics and flits!"

"Tics 'n flits 'n twitches, oh my!"

"Alice in Wonderland?"

"Wizard of Oz."

"Damn!" I broadly exclaimed, stepping free of her flamingo leg lock. "Do you see what you're doing to me? I'm losing complete control!"

"You've never been wrong before?"

"Of course."

"That's a relief. Nobody likes a know-it-a—"

"Seven years ago this past June. A Tuesday, I think. Overcast, threat of rain." Giggly, goofy, both silly with laughter, she grabbed my shirt, yanking me to her.

There should be an understood rule about frolicking fools attempting to lip lock. In a word, don't! Why? Because in the heat of silliness, something is bound to go wrong, and moments remembered sliding on soft, moist, dew dipped lips, will have to be cached away, a memorable memory. We learned the hard way when, with mouths stretched taut from grins and giggles, we joined, met, no, collided, better yet, smashed together, fillings shifting, as enamel hard bone met enamel hard bone!

It was a 'dead' sound, a dead, hollow bone sound. The same sound heard in museums in the pre-dawn hours, when amorous skeletons mate. What? That's right! City dwellers think it the noise of early morning trash men. Surprise!

As sudden as we hit, so weren't we as quick to back away.

Jodi yelped, covering her bloody upper lip. My hand flew to my mouth, grabbing what I knew was a loose front tooth. Covering my mouth was a small blessing as I smothered a pained, smut laden tirade, raunchy enough to make the devil blush!

"We can't go on like thith," Jodi sputtered, "thomebody'th going to get hurt!" She tried desperately not to laugh, to not tear the wound wider than it was.

"Too late, wouldn't you say? Besides, this is going well," I said, chuckling through the pain.

"Going well? What are you, mathochithtic?"

"What? Oh, masochistic? No. I've had my fair share of snooty, boring girlfriends, and believe me," I went on, running cold water on a paper towel, "in no way do you even come close to that category. You're in a class all by yourself." I smiled, dabbing blood from her lip.

"Really?" She grinned, reaching to touch my face, my jaw, my lip, my tooth.

"Yep, you're in a special class." I swallowed back a chuckle, realizing what I had said.

Jodi gripped the tooth, knowing I neither could, nor would, move. "No, what you thaid about thnooty, boring girlfriendth."

"Yes, you're no'."

"I'm not?"

"No."

Scowling she asked, "Who ith?"

"Le' go an I'll wri'e you ou' a lis', if you wan'," I offered in jest. She did.

"Penthil," she said, snatching one off the counter.

"You don't really . . ." I began to ask, when she motioned to grab my tooth once more. I dodged away, asking, "Why would you want a list of past snooty, bor—"

"I don't."

"Huh?" I scowled, completely lost.

"I want a litht of your prethent girlfriendth."

I know I could lose my way out of a walk-in closet, but I couldn't have been any more lost and confused than at that moment. *'Why would she want . . .'* then, *'Oh-h!'* Confusion cleared.

I gave one last dab at a trickle of blood from Jodi's lip, tore a clean paper towel free, and took the pencil. Ready to write, I stopped. "You're sure you need a list?" She looked to me expression free. Cupping my hand so she could not see, my pencil wrote, and wrote, and wrote, stopped, then wrote some more, or so she thought. I handed her the list.

"Jodi," was all she read, all I wrote.

'flit'

'tic'

-7-

'Kiss My Face'

"Try it. The swelling's gone down."

"She sells seashells down by the seashore."

"Much better."

Between helping Jodi ice down her lip, fussing with my tooth, and responding ever so gentle, ever so willing to each and every 'tic', about twelve-thirty, one o'clock, I proudly announced, "Brunchfest is served."

Sitting across from her at the kitchen table, I caught myself smiling, grinning at nothing special, just getting an odd kick out of watching her eat. We could be talking about the curious timeline between toenail and hair growth, not that we did, or the economic collapse of Prussia, not that we had, not that we would, and I'd find myself smiling, grinning, giddy as a loon. I had no doubt in my mind, no doubt whatsoever, if I saw her floss, I'd get a chubby!

"I have something to tell you," Jodi said, an almost grave tone in her voice.

"Do tell."

"Last night, at the show," she began, pausing to clear her throat, "some of those kids—"

"Yes?"

"Well, a few are mine."

Struck dumb, my flitting brow promptly cured, "A few?" I chirped. "How many are a few?"

"Well, do you remember seeing two sets of twins?"

"Twins? Yes. Cute. Don't tell me," hoping I was joking, "one set is yours?"

"No."

"Whew!"

"Both are."

"You have two sets of . . . four chil—"

"And the set of triplets?"

"Triplets! Seven of those kids are yours?" I gulped in disbelief.

Finger counting, "No," she paused, "nine altogether." I coughed up a bit of scrambled delicacy.

"Nine! How? I mean, I know how . . . nine?" A fly, apparently thinking my gaping maw a good spot to nap, flew in; roughage! "I had no idea!"

"How could you? I never mentioned it."

"If you're never told, whattya know?"

"What?"

"Nothing. An old family saying."

"At two o'clock, I have a date with the other seventeen. So, I'm sorry, but I have to go."

"What?!? Wait!" I blurted. "That's impos . . . sevente . . . twenty-six rugrats?"

"I admit, I do have my share, but you've got to love them."

"You maybe!" Jodi looked at me, expressionless. "Wait a second. You run a nursery!"

"No."

"Like a Humpty-Dumpty Day Care. Something like that, right?"

"No."

"No?"

There was a long pause, then, she broke, laughing. "Two down, one to go!"

Lost, shaking my head, all I could do was grin. "I have no idea."

"And, time is up. I win!" She laughed aloud. "I teach grades one thru three!"

Overwhelmed with relief, normal breathing returned, as did my brow flit. Knowing she'd set me up and I'd been had, hook, line and sinker, I had to laugh. I saw by the playful look on her face, she enjoyed her little ruse.

"That explains the wrong impression about the make-up."

"Wrong impression?"

"I enjoy doing make-up for the adult shows, but occasionally, I also do make-up for the kids. Once a month, we celebrate however many birthdays there are, by making a special day. We go on field trips, have Game Day, something special, a day just for them. Last night, I came straight from Make-up Day to your show."

"Make-up Day?"

"The girls have a ball. But, to get the boys to play along, I had to promise them Wrestling Day. The kids don't know it, but that's also STD Day."

"Sexually Transmit—"

"No, silly. Substitute Teacher Day."

"I never heard of such a thing."

"I know. I made it up!" Her hand slapped the table. "I was going to call it Headache Day, but I thought they'd catch on." Her laugh was infectious.

Everything was falling in place. It was not difficult to understand the link between Jodi's chosen profession and her personality; easygoing, yet assured, unassuming, funny, charming, with a kind, caring character. She was, as she often referenced, 'a big-boned woman-child' herself.

"See you later this week?"

"No," she softly said, "tomorrow. Kiss my face."

'tic'

As mentioned, *'But maybe, just maybe, if she could love, be loved, share love, as long, as hard, as true, as she could laugh, and near daily, as an extra added bonus, show me, teach me how, I will right now, after a lifetime of disbelief, recant, and atop the highest peak, on a stack of Bibles, swear to a caring, giving, merciful God!'*

In less than twelve hours I'd decided it was time to hire a sherpa, buy some Bibles, and take a hike!

'flit'

Because of our time spent last night, and at breakfast this morning, I felt I had known Jodi all my life. Even before she backed out of the driveway, I missed her. I was open to, found delight in, welcomed the thought, we were entering into the definitive 'whirlwind relationship'.

~~~

I'd see her in the morning, but Jodi would be busy with two shows, afternoon and evening, the entire week-end. As much as I missed her, *'The show must go on!'* I chuckled.

Checking the listings in the Boston Phoenix, I found an open mike for that night at a coffeehouse in Cambridge. Knowing nothing about artsy-fartsy Cambridge, I called ahead for directions. "Sign-up by nine, ten minute stage limit."

'You want to make a difference in New York?' I questioned myself. *'This is the way it has to be for the next few weeks. Grab whatever stage time you can, whenever, wherever you can.'*

I spent the afternoon going over and over the material. Knowing Jodi was not available to do make-up, I had to rethink, revise, totally strip away the 'eye' impact. Now, but for mannerisms and body language, visually it would be a stool, my can of Right Gua . . . er . . . a microphone, and the music. No rocker, no robe, slippers, or make-up, nothing to hide behind.

Until I could again present the material how I envisioned, approval now rested solely on 'ear' impact . . . the story.

~~~

It was a good hour or more, depending on downtown Boston traffic, to the room. On the drive, I couldn't stop assessing last night. *'Overall, I may not be thrilled with the comments, rather the lack of. Still, the judging powers-that-be said I won and I did bring home a trophy. Well, maybe not the biggest trophy, but at least I took one with a centered nameplate . . . it's the little things. And, though my long fantasized night with Shirley seemed a complete and utter disaster, I can't dismiss it totally. After all, there was an ample amount of nippleage. And, knowing the difference twixt paranoid and convinced, I am certain Raymond, given the opportunity, would take great pleasure in jumping from a dark crevice, pummeling the living bejesus outta me! Then, there's Jodi.'* After all is said and done, there's Jodi. *'Lucky dog! Lucky, lucky, lucky dog!'*

~~~

Giving just due, with its many theatres, art galleries, and espresso cafes, *'Upscale Cambridge is just the place to bring this material,'* I assured myself.

As I climbed the stairs, I walked past a spattering of 'earthy' folks, into a dark, intimate, smoke and incense filled room. Intimate, as in seating for about thirty. Dark, as in 'if not for the occasional table candles, I wouldn't see a hand in front of me' dark! The smell of Mother Nature's finest hung so heavy in the room, a contact high was a given for one and all.

"First time here? The stage order is the same as the sign-up list," said a Bob Dylan wannabe, sitting near-by.

"Thanks." I sat, hunkered over candlelight, signing up. "I'm ninth."

"Unless you want to be first."

"Anything but first," I said in mock jest, my butterflies flapping, agreeing.

"If no one goes first, shall we ever begin?" Philosophy 101. Cambridge. Aka . . . Yogi Berraism.

"If your nose runs, and your feet smell, you're built upside down." I chuckled. "Or something like that."

"Yeah, something like that." He was more an internal chuckler. "What's that?" he asked.

"Cassette player."

"I don't like being recorded."

"Oh, no, I'm not . . ." *When you fell off your high-horse, did you land on your head? Why would I . . .* ' "This is for me. Pre-taped music. Instrumental."

"You're not going to get anywhere in the business working off other people's music."

"You're right, but they are my words."

"Even so, half the package belongs to someone else. I've been in this business twelve years. Unless you learn to accompany yourself, you're just spinning your wheels."

"For now, this is what I have."

"Have it your way."

Later in the evening my self-appointed mentor took the stage. His allotted ten minute set consisted of original music and lyrics. That is, originally written by Jerry Jeff Walker, James Taylor, and of course, Bob Dylan.

At times I have to ask, "Is it me?"

I tormented myself as number nine loomed. *I'm sending up something they've never heard, but delivered with conviction, if I believe in the story, they'll never notice I took the stage with a recorder, right? They'll overlook I'm talking, telling a story, not singing, right? Right?'* I tried convincing myself. *'Right, and the Pope's a family man!'*

"Let's give a nice hand for . . . can we buy more lights? Number nine," said the host.

Grabbing a stool to place the recorder on, I made my way to the postage stamp stage, stepping on a minimum of toes and some poor bugger's foot. I placed the stool with recorder on it next to me, and sat on the already set stage stool, my finger at the ready on the 'Play' button. From my new vantage point, I looked out at the eerie sight of the room, the occasional ghoulish face lit by flicking candlelight. In jest, to break the ice, I asked, "Anybody got a match?"

Silence.

"Not since Superman died!" came the retort, and spattering of guffaws.

"Proof, kryptonite's not the gift for everyone!" Not so much as a chuckle came back. At moments like this, the Post Office seemed a nice place to be . . . forever and ever! "I won't take but three minutes of your time. I've written something and I'd like your opinions. Please, be kind," I offered, smiling, though more serious than not. The response was a scattering of titters. *'If this works, free stamps for everyone!'*

I pressed 'Play', knowing there was a five second leader of tape before the music began, and waited.

Seven seconds.

Eleven seconds.

Fifteen . . .

Figuring I'd overlooked pre-setting the sound, I fiddled with the volume control.

Nothing.

Looking down at the recorder, not able to see a thing, I picked it up. Holding it a scant inch or two from my face, looking in the little window, I saw the tape spinning 'Fast Forward' like a bat outta hell!

Feeling for the 'Stop' button, I pressed.

'Eject.'

Shoving the cassette back in the tray, I pressed the 'Rewind' button. "Sorry, bear with me." I heard the tape stop. "I have it now," I assured the gathering. Taking my lighter out, flicking a quick flame, I hit 'Stop' then set my finger on 'Play'.

Whether being respectful and smothering a laugh, guffawing outright, or shaking their heads at my bumbling, I know there had to be some who thought this was rehearsed. One thing for sure, judging by their stares, I had their attention!

Trying to save the moment, I said in self-depreciating jest, "I won't be back again, I promise." This was received with applause, the applause I'd hoped for since walking on stage, but when I was done! Not before I'd begun!

My entire being now consisted of one frazzled nerve!

'Play' button finger ready, I prayed for a 'Vanish' button. "Without further ado . . ."

"Wanna bet?" Not waiting for the laughs to die down, I hit 'Play'.

Think of the many times you've heard 'Auld Lang Syne'. Now take the first two lines, 'Should auld acquaintance be forgot, and never brought to mind? Should auld acquaintance be forgot, and days of o' lang syne?' and forget them.

Think, music.

Hear, Guy Lombardo and his orchestra.

Now, imagine the music, just the music . . . those twenty-seven opening morose notes, *BLARING* at you! Because, forgetting to turn the 'Volume' control back down after fiddling with it, that's just what was heard!

Once again, as if hearing this slice of winter holiday cheer on a leftover, humid, summer type night in mid-September wasn't weird enough, this group has also to contend with the extremely loud, sharp, brittle tone of a cheap recorder! I was both mesmerized and awed as I watched those eerie, ghoulish, candle lit faces, turn startled and distorted! People jumped and twitched, flinching at the sudden, grating, disturbing intrusion!

To save face, I thought to hit 'Stop' and start all over again. The audience, I knew, for obvious reasons, would have no patience for this. It did occur to me to take the recorder in hand and just leave, but, humiliating as it may be, this was not a viable option either. *'The show must go on!'* Believe me, with all due respect, even hardcore theatre enthusiasts have to trust me on this, there are times, *'The show must go on!'* is just plain wrong!

Though feeling I had started late, I went on with the telling anyway, rushing words together while fumbling to adjust the 'Volume' down. Hitting the exact notes with the right words, trying to catch the story up to the music, was an impossible task. Quick to think ahead, I dropped an entire line, jumping forward in the story, hoping I would hit a stride of musical note and spoken word. Not until I reached the mental splice, did I realize I had jumped too far ahead in the story

I ran out of words well before the music came to a final notes end. I can put it no other way than to say, the crowd just stared. As I gathered up the recorder, "Sorry, it's just not my night," was all I could think to say.

Not able to leave well enough alone, a pasty-faced female with a very long braid, wearing sandals, puffy blouse, and peasant dress, the universal get-up for love, peace, and understanding, chimes up, "That's showbiz, Bucko!"

As much as I wanted to say, *'Kiss my . . . '* I thought of Jodi, thinking, *'face.'* Saying, "You're right. That's showbiz," I walked off.

I've heard it said, *'The worst performers are those ill-prepared.'* The next worst? Those not willing to concede their three, five, or ten minutes are simply not working! Get off!

Two, maybe three people, offered very thin, even embarrassing, applause. Making my way to the exit door, I tried not making toe, foot, or eye contact. *'Get out the door, get in the car, just get out of here,'* was all I could think.

Near escaping, I heard, "At least get a guitar case," from my Bob Dylan wannabe mentor.

'What the hell's that supposed to mean?' Wanting to say, 'Up yours, smart ass!' again I thought best keeping to myself and walked out.

～～～

"Then I came home." The details of my nightmare told the next morning, I handed Jodi a tissue.

"At least get a guitar case!" she snorted, dribbling her coffee, wiping her tear filled eyes.

"That's not funny!" I had to laugh through my playful scolding. "More coffee? After what I put them through, compared to what he, or anyone else could have said, I got off pretty easy. Did you have breakfast yet? The ironic thing is, not one of the tunes he did was writ—"

"He's right."

"What? He's right? Didn't you hear me? Not one thing he did was original."

"What's that to do with you?"

"Well, it just seems he . . . his music wasn't his eith—"

"And? Again, what's that to you?"

"What?"

"Until we get to New York, know what you should do?" There was a long pause. I stood looking at her, waiting for the answer, growing a bit impatient. Finally, with a playful grin, she said, "Say, 'What?'"

'Huh?' "What?"

"Get a guitar case."

"For what? To carry my lunch in? I don't mean to be rude, but you don't listen very well, because you didn't hear me at all! Sorry. How did your shows go yesterday?"

"You didn't hear me at all!" she mimicked, ignoring my change of subject.

"What are you talking about? Listen, I don't play!"

"Listen, I don't care!"

"Are you like this often?" I asked, with an edgy grin. "Cause you're not making any sen—"

"Most of the other people play guitar, right?"

"Yes."

"Some of them take their guitar to the stage, still in the case, right?"

"Some."

"Get a guitar case and put the recorder in it." She beamed.

"But—"

"Those nights when I'm not there, when you do it without the make-up and all . . . use the guitar case. The crowd doesn't know what the crowd doesn't know."

"But they will!"

"Yes, when you're ready to tell them. Mislead them somehow. Tell a joke."

"A joke?"

"Yes. Lead them into it."

'A joke.'

~~~

"Next up, number . . ." said the host.

As I stood, "This'll work, right?" I whispered to Jodi.

She looked me square in the eye and smiled. 'tic'

I stood at the mike, grasping the handle of my new, old, time worn, twenty-dollar guitar case.

"Happy to be here this evening, very special night for me. Not only do I get to spend a few minutes with you folks, but tonight, I'm celebrating, five years of marriage." I made a small bow, taking in the polite applause. "Yeah, five years ago tonight my ex-wife remarried; I've been celebrating all day!"

I set the case on the first stool, sat on the other, waiting for a fair number of laughs to fade.

Looking out at fifty/sixty friendly faces, "I have a story to share with you." And, as if I hit a mute button, the room hushed.

I undid the remaining case latch . . .

'snap'

. . . glanced at Jodi . . .

'tic'

. . . set my finger on 'Play' . . .

'click'

. . . and the music began. Sans make-up, robe, and slippers, there I sat, barefaced. I closed my eyes, and with minimum old character hand movement and body language, in a mellow, moody, aged voice, I told my story, every word, first to last. For three minutes, not a sound, not a noise, not a peep was heard, nothing, but the rise and fall of the story's emotional peaks and valleys . . . to fade of the last note.

And applause.

'flit'

~8~

'Gymnasties!'

Three weeks had slipped by. One month 'til a New York stage.

'Scared?' I'd inquire of me. *'No.'*

Then lose myself imagining the night.

'How about now?'

~~~

Despite demands on her time; teaching during the day, requests for her make-up artistry in the evening, when she couldn't be at my little shows, Jodi and her 'tic' were with me in spirit.

Her joke idea, plus placing the recorder in a beat up guitar case, worked most of the time, not every time, but more often than not.

The audiences I found to try my story, to prepare for New York, were more at ease, open and receptive, thanks to Jodi.

On Thursday nights after work, I'd stop at the local market, buy the Boston Phoenix, the weekly alternative news, and start all over again making phone calls, lining up stage time for the upcoming week. An ad in one edition caught my eye, piqued my curiosity, yielding an unexpected adventure.

'Actors Wanted!' read the ad in the Theatre section. 'All ages, colors, shapes & sizes. One day. Paid! Auditions by appt.' Closing with a phone number.

'Paid, hm? One day. Paid.'

Dialing the number, all I could think was, *'They're gonna put me in the movies . . .* '"Hi. I'm calling on the ad in the Phoenix. Yes. Who? Mr. Pop . . . Popodopod . . . yes, I'll hold." *They're gonna make a big star out of me . . .* '"Eleven. Larger or smaller. Really? Three hundred dollars? Some stage, no film." *'Make a film about a man that's sad and lonely . . .* '"Sunday at two. Room 302. Harold Johnson, Cambridge. Thank you." *'All I gotta do is act natur . . . Jodi!'*

Paid!

'Won't she be surprised!'

~~~

"You need a resume," coached Jodi.

"Pretty thin resume. A walk-on in a community production."

"Well, elaborate on the coffeehouse shows, New York and all. How about headshots?"

"There's my yearbook picture."

"High school? That's it? I think it's a little dated."

"But a very good shot if I do say so myself, and—"

"And you do!" she chided. "Do you have a camera?"

"Yes."

"Alright. Get the camera. I'll take some pictures. It's Thursday. I'll drop the roll off in the morning, have the pictures rush processed, and back by Saturday. They won't be nine-by-twelve, but at least you'll have something."

"You are good, you know that?"

"No, you are."

'flit'

"No, you are."

'tic'

"No, you are."

"No, you . . ." We could keep this up so long, my molars would ache.

"Ain't love grand?"

"Isn't."

"Is too!" More often than not, I caught myself gazing at Jodi when we were together, thinking about her when I was alone. *'Easy to smile, to laugh. Easy to be with, to hold, to lov—'*

"What?" she asked, a quizzical smile.

"What are you doing?"

"When?"

"Forever?"

'tic'

'flit'

~~~

click . . . click, click, click, click

"Enough."

"One more." Jodi smiled playfully. "Take your shirt off!"

"I don't think they need a photo of me half naked."

"Might, if it's a beach shoot. Could be why they asked for all shapes and sizes."

"Maybe it's a mob scene, like those old battle movies, when Attila the Hun crests the horizon with a million Hun warriors!"

"Hon, take off your shirt."

"Maybe you should take a picture of my feet."

"Why?"

"He asked what size feet I had."

"Why?"

"I don't know, but he laughed when I said eleven. He laughed even harder when I said, if it meant getting paid, I could be larger or smaller."

"Maybe it's a running movie, like the Boston Marathon. Well, you made an impression. At least he has a sense of humor. Take your shirt off."

"Boy, when you get on a kick." Then, with a coy smile, "You first," I suggested.

"No, you."

"No, you."

"No, you."

I'll just say, giddy, we playfully 'clicked' the night away. I'd show photos, but unfortunately, or fortunately, after the first few shots, we ran out of film.

~~~

Jodi came through with the photos, she also helped puff up my first theatre/film resume, but because of our conflicting Saturday schedules, I wasn't able to get everything until Sunday, on my way out. Having to pick-up the photos, go back to Cambridge for the audition, and not knowing my way around, I left at twelve-thirty for the two o'clock meeting. Finding the hotel was no problem, but my car was not running up to snuff, so I arrived twenty minutes late.

Running through the lobby, I willed the elevator doors open, pressing three.

"Mr. Popoodopo . . ." I asked of the stubby, sweaty, no neck, balding man, sitting on the hall settee, outside room 302.

He nodded. "Popodopoulis. You must be—"

"Yes. I'm your two o'clock. Sorry I'm late. My car's not what it use—"

"Not to worry. I have one other meeting at three." My gut feeling of all not being on the up 'n up was justified when, setting the resume aside, he lingered on the photos. "This all you have?"

"My headshots are on re-order," I lied.

"No, I mean, do you have more photos?"

"That's it. We ran out of film."

"We?"

"My girlfriend did the shoot." And at that, all apprehension disappeared. "So, three hundred dollars for one day? What exactly is this film about?"

"It's not a film."

"Alright, the movie?"

"It's not a movie."

"Then what the . . ." Sensing the MGM lion would not be making an appearance in the opening credits, all apprehension reappeared.

"It's a flick."

"A 'flick'." *'Okay. Mr. Movie Maker likes to make 'flicks'.* "What kind of 'flick'?" *'Why is it I know right where this is going?'*

"It's a comedy." Suddenly relieved, *'What the hell was I thinking?'* "I call it 'Gymnasties'." *'Great title!'* I snorted. Then, "It's a skin flick." And there it was! *'Well shut my mouth!'* I can't say I didn't expect it, but it sure as hell made me laugh when I heard it!

"Are you serious?"

"Are you interested?"

"Three hundred dollars?" I thought, too loud. "I mean no, no thanks."

In a matter of fact tone, he said, "I was asking, not casting," and shrugged.

"Right. Well, I, uh, anyway . . ." I stammered, standing. Whether by design or accident, but not immediately noticed by me, when he picked up my resume setting beside him, a nine by twelve, black and white headshot came with it.

"Here," he said, handing my photos and resume back. Blame it on the sweat trailing down his face and neck, the matted, wet, fine curly hairs rimming his head, or the pathetic air which suddenly loomed, but I just could not bring myself to extend a handshake. Caught in an awkward moment, I nodded and turned, heading back to the elevator. The seconds, standing nose to elevator doors, seemed to pass like hours. I know he heard me cursing the motionless doors under my breath. To not seem nonplussed, to do something, anything to ignore the air, I shuffled the photos and resume. It was then I spied the headshot.

"Oh, that's not yours," he said.

'She's not yours either, buddy!' I chuckled to myself, as the doors opened. "She's very attractive," I said, first because she was; and second, it was the only thing I could think to say. "Is she the—"

"That's her."

"Uh-huh. You've worked with her before?" I asked, as the doors closed.

"No, she's new."

"Hmmph, well, here you go." I handed back the picture. "Good luck," and turned away. Back again, staring at the doors, somehow I knew he knew I was going to ask at least one more question, so, "How do you know she'll show up?"

"Her day is bought and paid for."

"Yeah, but—"

"She'll show."

"You're sure? What is she . . . a hooker?"

"Not at all. No different than you. New to the business, looking for a break."

"Yeah, but porn?"

"Pays the bills. You still have to eat. Oh, uh, you might want to press the button. Tell you what," he said, extending his card, "leave your resume and take this, in case you change your mind."

"Four hundred for the day."

He paused, eyeing me. "Maybe, three-fifty."

"That wasn't a question." The elevator doors finally opened. One resume short, one questionable business card heavier, I stepped in.

~~~

Approaching the entrance ramp to the Southeast Expressway, for my long trip home, my car, apparently deciding it had been pushed just about enough, became possessed; smoking, banging, pooping and coughing. *'No, no, not now!'* My buggy simply stopped running. *'I'll be a son-of-a—!'* I coasted to the roadside, locked up, and started walking.

'Why? Why me? Was it something I said? Something I did? Something I said I did? Did I do a really, really, bad deed in another life to piss you off? Because, it seems I'm being taken to task for something! If this has to do with asking for four hundred dollars to do the fil . . . flick, I was joking! I have no intention! Why don't you go pick on someone else! I'm tired!'

~~~

Not 'til six-thirty, seven, after I'd found a garage, had the car towed, made my way back to the highway, and hitchhiked home, did I finally collapse on the sofa. Jodi had stopped by earlier, leaving dinner and a note on the kitchen table, with a phone number where she could be reached.

"Hey, good lookin'." I stroked the one bright spot in my otherwise dismal day.

"Hi, movie star. Can I have your autograph?" I know she was smiling, I could sense its comfort over the phone lines. A simple smile, but so capable of snapping me out of a dark mood, from self-wallowing doldrums.

"You're not going to believe the day I've had. First, well, not first, but if you come over, you won't see my car. Stop anyway. I'm here, the car's not; broke down in Boston. It's going to cost a small fortune to fix. I'm thinking about selling a body part. What's a healthy lung fetch? As far as the audition, it didn't go very well. To tell you the truth, it's not quite . . . what? You spoke to him? What time were you here? Well, it's not about the Boston Marathon, or running laps, I can assure you that! More like lapping runners! It's por . . . he said what? Four hundred dollars! Poor? I said, poor? Oh, poor, no, no, the script . . . poor script, but it has potential. He actually said four hundred dollars? For one day? No mistake? Yeah, that would be a little hard to turn down. I'll sleep on it . . . we'll talk tomorrow. What? Now? I have his card. You think I should? Yeah, money's money. Okay, see you tomorrow. Me too. What? No, I'm pretty sure I'll be doing my own stunts. No, yeah, you're right. Gotta start somewhere. Bye."

The call to Popodopoulis was brief, but sure enough, one day, eight hours, nine to five. I was to meet the crew and female lead at a beachfront bungalow, north of Boston, Monday. I had three days to back out.

'Tomorrow, when I tell Jodi what she gave me the green light to do, she's going to laugh herself silly! Getting paid, getting laid!' I shook my head in disbelief, grinning at how today's events unfolded. *'I should hire a crew just to film her expression! Ha! I wouldn't miss this for anything!'*

~~~

"Convertible, yes. Clean faulty fuel injectors, rebuild carburetor, adjust tappets, replace alternator, starter, and (to stop a quart-a-day oil leak) pull and replace manifold gaskets. How much? One fifty, one seventy-five? That's not all that bad . . . oh, right, parts. Plus, one seventy-five, two twenty-five, labor. Don't really have a choice, do I? There's a small tear in the top. Can you? Yeah? How much? I don't think so! How about a piece of duct tape? Must be good duct tape! Nothing. Sure, what the hell!"

'Oh, you are a tricky li'l devil, aren't you?'

~~~

"Keys?" I questioned, as Jodi set them on the table. "What are those for?"

"For you."

"Me?"

"I'm working two shows for three more weeks. You can't walk to the shoot, so take my car."

"Oh, yeah, the film. I've thought it over and, well, I'm going to take a pass."

"You've got to be kidding! You get cast in your first film, getting paid better than union scale to romp on the beach, surrounded by an entire crew of doters and go-fers, and you're having second thoughts?" I couldn't help my playful grin, thinking about the shock Jodi had coming. "Are you serious about this or not?"

"I am, but—" I decided the time had come to level with her.

"No, no buts!"

"That's what you think," I mumbled. I had to tell her the truth.

"Buts aside—"

"Easier said than—" and I would tell her, as soon as I could get a word in.

"Want to know what I think?"

'Soon' never seemed so far away! "Jodi, sh-h. Listen close. *Gymnasties!*'

After considering it for a second, "Catchy title," she said, and she was off again. "This is all new to you. Everyone on site is going to know this is your first film. Smile a lot. Ease yourself in, that's your first move."

"Ease myself—"

"Then, when you're comfortable, spread out, make a little wiggle room. Move around."

'*Wigg*—' If pent up, unreleased laughter were a gas, I would surely explode!

"Nerves, that's all it is. You're scared, and you should be. Think about your first time on stage," she reasoned. "But for a handful of memorized lines, you were bare to the world."

"I never did 'Hair!'" And at that, I burst. Jodi just stared.

"Maybe it's time you pulled yourself up by your bootstraps and—
"

"Suppose I'm not wearing any?"

Weary, she snatched her keys, and turned for the door. "Call when you're serious!"

"Jodi, stop! It's porn!"

"Of course it is! What have we been talking about?"

"No, you don't understand. The film's not a film. It's a flick! Gymnasties! Gym-*nasties*! Get it?"

After a long pause, and empty stare, Jodi simply asked, "A comedy, right?"

"No, it's, I mean, yes, it's supposed to be a comedy!"

"Sounds funny."

"Listen, listen close. I was cast in a flick! A skin flick! For real!"

"I know! Isn't it great? I bet you'll be funny."

"Jodi, it's porn! Porn! Porn! Porn! Porn!"

"And?"

"And, um, I don't . . . there's a lot of trampoline stuff going on. What do you mean, 'and'?"

"And, what's the problem? You never played on a trampoline?"

"Tell me, repeat to me one thing I just said."

"Something about a trampoline, gymnastics—"

"*Gymnasties! Gymnasties!* Pornography! *A SKIN FLICK WANKER FILM!*" Exasperated, "Doesn't any of this bother you just a little bit?"

"Well, yeah."

"Well, thank you! Thank you very much!"

"What's bothering you?"

"What's bothering me? No, you tell me what's bothering you!"

"Nothing. You do what you have to do."

"But I don't want to!"

"Of course you do!" She laughed, but with a comical scowl.

"No, I don't!"

"Why?"

"They're the worst of the worst! Poor filming, bad acting, and you can forget about the storyline! Obviously, you've never seen one or you'd know."

"I saw one. Something to do with a fairy tale Princess—"

"We're talking hardcore porn."

"And a donkey. Actually, the donkey was a handsome Prince who had a spell cast on him by the evil bitch. The only way the spell could be broken was if the donkey bonked the Princess."

"Bonked?"

"You know, the donkey had to convince the Princess to—"

"I know what the donkey had to convince the Princess to do!"

"It wasn't pretty."

"What has any of this got to do with New York?"

"Oh, now I see why you're upset. You think this, this opportunity, is beneath you, excuse the pun. Well, you're right, it is, but this has nothing to do with New York. Sometimes you have to take a sharp left to get back to center again. It's like all part of a bigger plan."

"What are you talking about . . . opportunity?"

"You've heard of 'Rocky' right? The movie? Well, Sylvester Stallone, the guy who stars in it, also wrote it. His first role was in a porn movie; 'Party at Kitty and Studs', it came out a few years ago, 1970 I think. Anyway, he was struggling, looking for a break, just like you. And do you know what he was paid for doing the entire shoot? Two hundred dollars! He took the name 'Italian Stallion', did the film, took the money; look at him now. It's all opportunity . . . you have to take advantage of any opportunity."

"Look, I'm no Stallone, and I do not call parading my arse around on the big screen, a hundred times bigger than it is, an opportunity!"

"Are you Irish?"

"No, why?"

"Arse. I think that's Irish for ass. Anyway, I think you have a filmable ass . . . arse."

Then came the dawn. "Oh-h, I get it. I see what you're doing. 'Now I see,' said the blind man, to his dog with no ears! Now I get it. You had me going there for a minute. You're controlling the situation by doing just the opposite of what I would expect."

"Mm, no."

"Sure you are, and very good, too. If I say I'm going to do it, I lose, because then you'll get all upset at me for even thinking about doing such a thing. If I say I'm not going to do it, I lose, because you pretend to be upset, baiting me even more by calling, referring to this as an 'opportunity'!"

"It is."

"Uh-huh, right, but here's where the bottom of your little game drops out; it doesn't matter what choice I make, I can't go anywhere, any how, anyway, because I don't have a car! And, no matter how much I pretend I do, you and I both know I don't!"

"Stop me if . . . I'm just trying to understand. You don't want my *pretend* keys to use my *pretend* car? Or, did you want me to *pretend* I lost my keys? No, I have a better one . . . how about I *pretend* I don't even own a car, so I can *pretend* I like asking for rides, then you can *pretend* I don't even exist?"

"Look me square in the eye and tell me, your boyfriend, you, in all honesty, would not be upset if I did this."

She looked at me in a way she never had. "Please, do not put me there." There was a pause, a pause just long enough for me to understand, this wasn't her decision to make. "How much to get your car repaired?"

"About four hundred dollars."

Her jaw dropped. "Four hun . . . I know my mechanic would have charged less!"

"Kind of late now, don't you think?"

"Anyway, how much will you make for one day?"

"Four hun—"

'tic'

'flit'

Decisions, decisions, deci—

'Oh, shut-up!'

~9~

'Fluffer Knockers'

I am not going to waste good time discussing, debating, prattling on and on, about the many varied and valid, *'Reasons I Will Never Do Porn!'* which, believe me, are the very same reasons I share with most of you. The myriad of blatant wrongs in doing this so-called 'project', I wholeheartedly concur, far outweigh the rights.

And I'm not going to sit here and pretend I, like some of you, were not a bit taken aback by Jodi's seeming lack of good judgment, of prudence, for not taking the moral high road on the matter. However, to know her is to understand and, in all honesty, after awhile Jodi's take on the matter made 'practical' sense, if strictly from a monetary standpoint.

Now, obvious arguments aside, what you must know is, despite having third, fourth, one hundred sixty-nine, as many as five hundred ninety-seven second thoughts on the 'why and why not' of the matter, I'm far from being a prude. But, between life's giving and getting, needing and wanting, 'twixt and 'tween, my choices of *'Do it! Don't do it!'* along with a nagging neutral area of *'Eh, what the hell, why not!'* made for a sleepless night before.

~~~

'I have Popodopolopo, whatever's, number. One call, that's all it would take.'

Peter Principle.

'Hello, Mr. Popohead? Yes, I won't be making it today. Well, to be honest, this goes against every fiber of my being! Good-bye!'

Doug Dong.

'Hi. I can't, uh, my cat's not doing well. Yes. No, my cat! Scoliosis. I feel terrible. Bye.'

Dick B. Nimble.

'Sorry, but I have this 'thing' about strutting naked around strangers . . . about strutting around naked, period! Now that I think of it, I have this thing about strutting!

'E. Norm Ous.

'Hi, Mr. P. Listen, I have a great idea. How about if I had black balloons strategically taped over my privates? It'd still be porn, but with an artsy-fartsy touch. No? Burlesque is dead? Oh.'

Willy Wanka.

'Enough! I'm pulling over to the first phone booth I see. There's one. The party's over!'

Fiddle D. Dee.

'What? What are you kids laughing at? Got a problem? Put the BB gun down! You never saw a grown man in an orange clown car before? Stop pointing! You shoot me and you'll be crapping BBs for a month!'

Tricky Dicky.

'Where in hell's a phone? There has to be another phone. I can't do this! Why?'

Ben Dover.

'I can't think of a good porn name, that's why!'

Beaver Cleaver.

'Hey! Hm? No!'

~~~

'There's the house, right on the beach, just like what's-his-name said. I'll park way over here. Maybe there's a payphone between here and the front door.' The idea made me groan. *'You're at the beach, Einstein! No way in hell is a payphone going to suddenly appear!'* With each cautious step I eyeballed the house harder, certain a goon, ghost, goblin, or God Himself would smite me on the spot just for showing up!

'Every step is another part of your test, isn't it? How'm I doin'? Hello? Busy, or did you desert me, again? Fine, don't talk to me!'

Set about four feet high on a number of, what appeared to be, stubby telephone poles, the house was a typical beachfront bungalow. The site, the location itself, was postcard perfect, with nothing between the house and breaking waves but pristine sandy beach.

Unaware of anyone or anything, focused as I was on the house, hearing, "Can I help you?" startled me. I spun about to find a guy, about my age, toting two grocery bags.

"Hi. I'm look—"

123

"Oh, yeah, I saw your photo. You're the male talent. C'mon in. How's it goin'?"

"Fi—"

"I'm Ari."

"Ar—"

"Meet the production crew. Larry, Bob, Phil, Opie, Phillipe, Carl, Armand, Leopold, Denny, Les, Stephan, Ngo, this is . . ."

"Fr—"

"I have to go back out. I remembered paper towels, handy-wipes, mouthwash, ketchup, toothbrushes, floss, batteries, Saran Wrap, and kielbasa."

"What'dja forget?" asked a crewmember.

"Mints."

Though thinking, *'Gross!'* joking, I started to say, "Got to have min—"

"Words of a pro. What'd you say your name was?"

"Fr—" *'What's it matter?'* "Beaver Cleaver!" *'You're not listening to me anyway.'* The crew laughed. "What's the kielbasa for?" More laughter.

"Take a look around. Get comfortable. You need anything?"

"N—"

"When I get back we can get this show on the road." Ari left, leaving me standing there.

Along with a few obligatory nods and mumbled hellos, I know I picked up on some snickering. But it was the staring, the feeling of being sized up; of them thinking whatever they were thinking that did me in. Overwhelmed with a bout of nervous anxiety, wishing I had never taken this step, feeling like a raw kielbasa link, I turned, retreating after Ari, catching him as he was about to drive off.

He sensed something was wrong immediately because, when he rolled down his window, he shoved a notebook at me, saying, "While you're waiting, I could use your help. The script we were going to shoot from has been scrapped. I need some ideas . . . some bits. Whatever you can come up with would be great." And off he went.

'What? No Gymnasties? All right, what're you up to? It's all a game show with you, isn't it? What's going on up there?'

Caught between going or staying, I perched on the hood of Jodi's clown mobile and tried jotting some ide . . . bits.

~~~

(narrator)
Not long ago, I had my first UFO experience, up in East Bumphuck, Maine. How many remember their very first UFO experience? Raise 'em up! Raise 'em high! Anyone? No one? Shame! I was but a pimply-faced youth when I witnessed my first UFO . . . Unforgettable Female Orgasm!

'What the hell did you think I was talking about?'

~~~

My thoughts were hard pressed to flow, interrupted as I was, staring at the house, ignition keys in my pocket, thinking the situation over. *'Okay, give it one more hour, then see.'*

I walked back to the house, took a deep breath, stepped onto the wrap-around sun deck, took another deep breath, and went back in. There were three rooms, one large, two small, a kitchenette, and a bath. I noticed most of the furniture had been moved inside the smaller rooms. The one remaining piece, the focal point of crew interest was, of course, the king size bed.

I couldn't quite put my finger on it, but looking about, something struck me as odd. I must have been trying too hard to figure out what was bothering me because, from across the room, one of the crew asked, "Everything okay?"

All work came to a sudden halt. Though I'd caught numerous side-glances since walking back in, every eye was now directly on me. "Uh, yeah, sure. I was just, uh . . ." Not able to figure out fast enough what was rubbing me the wrong way, all I could think to say was, "Where's the trampoline?" From the looks and laughs, I was correct in assuming, no trampoline was to be had.

Now, I realize all beds become whatever couples want them to become from time to time, even trampolines. And, though I still couldn't see myself romping, flopping around in my birthday suit with a buck-naked woman I didn't even know, whether it be on a king size bed or not, to be honest, I felt a little disappointed there was not going to be a real trampoline!

Staying out of the way, I took a seat in a corner, looking busy, trying my hand at more bits.

~~~

We met via the East Bumphuck classifieds. 'Personality ++++' read her ad. I thought, 'Ah-ha . . . a schizophrenic!' She'd be all women . . . at one time or another!

She said her name was Rash . . . Matilda Rash. I suggested a name change . . . she opted for Rosie. She said she was a redhead. "My friends call me Red." 'Rosie Red Rash!' It didn't take long for her to get under my skin!

~~~

Watching the final touches being made to, on, about, and around the star of the show, the bed, the answer to what had been nagging me slowly became clear as the nose on my face; a video recorder, a camera, and two light poles. Set the lights, turn on the recorder, focus the camera, shoot. If need be, despite every one of the crew either holding, wrapping, plugging in, or pulling out a cable, certainly such a minimum amount of equipment could be handled by one person, let alone thirteen—the number of people, of guys, all guys, in this crew!

What I wanted to know; is this simply a matter of crew over-kill? Or, because they all appeared to be in their early to mid-twenties, was this a local college fraternity? A lusty, horny bunch that'd heard rumor of a porno shoot? Then again, could this be a meeting of Voyeurs Extraordinaire, attendance mandatory? In lieu of coffee and doughnuts—kielbasa!

"So, who does what?" I asked, to no one in particular.

Almost to a man, they answered, "Lights!"

'Thirteen guys to handle two lights? Yeah, and I'm John Holmes!'

I took a seat on the kitchen counter, attempting more bits.

~~~

By the time we met, she'd gone blonde. "A blonde, I am," she said. "A true blonde. A true blue blonde. A true blue blue-eyed blonde!" And she was. I know . . . I probed her iris.

She said she was a stripper at a nudist colony and began to cry.

~~~

"Anyone seen Mr. Popo . . ."

"You made it," said Popodopoulis, entering.

"Yes." He was sweaty, nervous, pre-occupied in thought; no different from our first meeting.

"You've met everyone?"

127

"I have. Well, not everyone."

"No? Who? Oh, the girl."

"Yes."

"She's on her way. Running late. She'll be here. Take it easy. Relax."

I admit I could have made good use of something to calm my stomach, but hearing 'relax' coming from him, a walking breakdown waiting to happen, well, it bordered a fine line between funny and insulting. "I'm okay."

"You're white as a ghost. Lets get somebody to slap some make-up on you."

'Slap?' Did he really say, *'Slap'?* Even if he said dab or apply, unless Jodi's hiding under the bed, make-up kit intact, nobody's going to *slap* anything anywhere! In fact, unless there's an emergency delivery of a newborn baby right there on the beach, and I get to be the hero slappee, *'I'd rather not hear the word 'slap' again today!'* "I need a little sun. I'll be outside."

~~~

Setting her breasts on the bar, Rosie said, "Look! Whattya think?"

Not wanting to upset her, "They're quite lovely," I said.

"What would you do if I told you they were enlarged with peanut oil?"

"All natural peanut oil extract . . . smooth not chunky?"

"Of course!"

"Well, I'd fill up your cleavage with Marshmallow Fluff, take two slices of Pumpernickel, place a slice of Pumpernickel on either side of each breast, then gently moosh 'em together. When the Marshmallow Fluff

*came oozing out I'd slowly . . . lick . . . and lick . . . and li . . . oh, I do
so love Fluffer-Knockers! But I've never given it much thought. Why?"*

~~~

Now I appreciate the axioms, truisms, having to do with 'bad things
happening to good people', as well as 'good things happening to
bad people', after all, fate does not discriminate. In this recent wake
of self-discovery, in looking at my life, my existence, more from an
open, creative, albeit skewed eye, I have come to realize I'm neither.
That is, I'm neither bad nor good; well, more good than bad. Though
I do seem to find myself dabbling, planting both feet up to my ankles
more one side of the fence than the other from time to time, I seem
to live in the middle, straddling the two.

This is why today's happening, I know it! *'I'm a straddler! That's it!
That's it in a nutshell!'* This is not a good thing. *'I can't do this. I'm
gone!'* What the hell was I thinking?

'Me? What was I thinking? What the hell were you thinking?'

How do people do it? Perform on cue? *'That's ridiculous!'* Money be
damned! What's with the ketchup? The kielb . . . *'I don't want to
know!'* Why did Jodi give me the green light to do this? *'I can't blame
her. She didn't negotiate, didn't drive me here.'* Jodi was just being her
practical self.

*'This . . . this is between you and me! You want to test me? Are you
waiting to see if I got the nads to go through with this? You want to see
me walk away? All right then, you watch! You just watch me! I'll go
. . . I'll go when I'm goddamn good and ready! Sorry, I am sorry, but
you really must admit you do have an annoying way of pushing people's
buttons!'*

~~~

*Rosie smiled. She had pearl drop teeth and ruby red gums. Poli-Grip
oozed from her upper plate. I'll never forget that smile. I'll never forget*

our very first date. We drove straight to the Hilltop Motel. She informs me, "Because of my religious beliefs I need a sign from above." So, I rolled down the hill, and there in the rearview mirror flashed the motel sign;
~~~ **LETOM** *~~~ LETOM ~~~* **LETOM** *~~~*

"The best sex I ever had was on the Riviera," she said. "Ever had sex on the Riviera?"

"No."

"Well, what're we waitin' for? Get on the hood!"

~~~

"Hey Beav, you sleeping?" asked Ari.

"Huh . . . wha . . . yeah . . . no," I mumbled. "Ready?"

"No."

"What time is it?"

"One, one-thirty. You okay? You don't look so good."

"I'm trying to get some color."

"Really? What are you going for? Crimson?"

Sitting up, leaning back on my elbows, I felt an uncomfortable tingle about my stomach, neck, back of my hands, and arms. Looking down to my feet, kicking off my sandals, I saw the wide angled strip of white skin the leather straps had hid from the sun. From there, up to my khaki shorts, my legs were red, not a crimson red . . . more a scarlet glow! Not having removed my shirt when I laid down, just unbuttoning, letting the sides fall away, parts of my stomach and chest, along with my exposed arms and face, felt like I had stood too near a bonfire! "Uh-oh, I think I'm done!"

"You never heard of sun block?"

To make matters all the worse; in preparing for this sunning session, I had set my hands, fingers slightly apart, on my stomach. It now appeared I was being 'belly-hugged' from behind! "There was nothing but clouds when I laid down," came my plea through clenched teeth, as I attempted, through the burn, to sit up.

"Uh-huh," was all he said, squinting at the sun.

"One-thirty? Really? Why didn't some . . . what's going on?"

"Nothing."

"I know. I can see that. Shouldn't there be?"

"I guess. I wouldn't be concerned."

"Did she get here yet?"

"Elora?"

"Whoever. God this hurts!" I grimaced. "So?"

"So . . . how do you like your kielbasa?"

~~~

To me, sex at that age was like a blessing. To Rosie, sex at any age was a blessing!

~~~

"'xcuse me?"

"Thought I'd fire-up the hibachi, make some lunch. How do you like your kielb—"

"Wait a minute. Where's Poopadoopa? The girl? I didn't come here to eat out!"

"Jot that down."

"Look, I just want to get this over with, get paid, and get out! This is a one shot deal here. Nobody said a thing about a second day!"

"Don't worry." He smirked, shrugged. "You'll get paid. We always do."

"You've done this before, I take it?"

"Sure, well, once. We ended up with enough Italian sausage to feed damn near the whole dorm! Tonight's kielbasa night." He laughed.

"So, you are students. I sort of figured."

"Money's money."

"Yeah, I've been hearing that a lot lately." I continued to jot bits down, trying to appear as cool, as nonchalant as possible. "Let me ask you something. Just out of curiosity . . . why the overkill?"

"It's a large dorm. Why?"

"Not the kielbasa! Why so many guys? Thirteen? Even two is one too many. One of you could do the entire shoot with no problem, but thirteen?"

"Are there that many? Really? Hmph, this is going to cost Pop a few bucks."

"He's paying everyone?"

"Well, yeah," Ari scowled. "You think we're . . . why else would we be here?"

"I don't know. I figured, all students, you came to see a . . . you know."

"To see a naked girl bounce around?"

"No! Well, yeah."

Ari laughed. "Did you see a trampoline?"

"No, but—"

He leaned in. "Listen, there's no girl, no shoot. All we have is kielbasa and, if you'd like some lunch, you'd better tell me how you like it."

~~~

We were getting pretty cozy when out of the blue, Rosie asked, "You like S&M?" Now, I don't know S&M from M&M, though I did once smoke an L&M, but tonight, I'm gonna find out! She tossed me this li'l towel, this li'l napkin, this li'l bib type thing, saying, "Get comfy. Put this on. This could get messy. I'll be right back."

'Heaven . . . I'm in heaven!' So, I'm lying there, naked as a jay-bird, the li'l towel, napkin, bib thing not doing anywhere near a good job covering Mr. Happy, when she walks back in carrying a plate. Lying there in my splendor, she bursts out laughing. I said, "What's the matter? You said S&M!"

"Yeah! Spaghetti and Meatballs!!"

~~~

Confused, not exactly clear what Ari was saying, I stopped writing. "What do mean 'there's no shoot'?"

"What's the problem? Don't you like kielbasa?"

Bewildered, I asked, "That's it?"

"Uh-huh. Now, I'm starved. About that kielb—"

"Can we skip the kielbasa for a minute?"

"It's good."

"I'm sure." Feeling a bit uneasy, I asked, "Where's Popo—"

"He went downtown. There's the glitch."

"Glitch?"

"If he finds a girl, the shoot is on."

"Finds? What's he doing? Picking some girl, any female, off the street?"

"Basically, yeah. Sounds kind of sordid the way you put it, but if—"

"How could it not sound sordid? It is sordid!"

"But, if he finds one, he'll pay her five hundred for the day, or what's left of it."

"Five hundred dollars? For the afternoon? I'm only getting four for the whole day!"

"Four? I'm only getting one-fifty!"

"Yeah, well, whatever . . . stay with me a minute on this, will you? Suppose he doesn't find a girl. I'll still get paid and I won't have to do a thing . . . nothing. Is that what you're telling me?"

"That's the way it worked last time."

~~~

Rosie's personalities grew. One day she says to me, "Snookie, I got that not so fresh feeling. Pick me up a six-pack." There we'd sit . . . me with my bottle of cheap wine . . . Rosie and her six-pack of Country Flowers. One night I grabbed the wrong bottle! To those familiar with Massengill's Extra Cleansing Country Flowers . . . add a shot of carbonation . . . tastes just like Ripple with a light bouquet!

~~~

"Last time?"

"Well, the only other time. Okay, keep this to yourself. About a year ago, Pop's visiting the dorm and he saw my equipment, *my film equipment,* asked if I'd like to make some money. It's just a handheld with a tripod, it was obvious he didn't know a Nikon from a Brownie, but he was impressed. Phillipe had the lights. We met him here, set everything up, ran cable for effect, and waited; the girl, whoever she was, never showed. Phillipe took a ride downtown with Pop, came back empty handed. Pop was pissed, but it wasn't our problem. He paid us in cash. The end. The way things look, the same thing is going to happen."

"Then, who's Elora?"

"Armand; his sister. Her husband's laid up, no insurance. They're on welfare with a couple of kids."

"So she goes to the interview, does a sexy little song 'n dance for Popo, gets the money in advance, but doesn't show. You guys occasionally lift a cable, get to spend a day at the beach, and make a few bucks. Is that about it?"

"Plus paper goods and toiletries."

"What?"

"Paper towels, handy-wipes, toothbrushes, toothpaste, floss, mouthwash, all the stuff I got at the store. Hey, I'm a college guy, not a Getty. Ketchup for the kielbasa, Saran Wrap for the leftovers. It's going to be a good week." Ari laughed, obviously pleased.

"Then the kielbasa and ketchup were not meant for anything other than—"

"Lunch. Why? What were you thinking?"

"Me? Uh, hey, sounds like a great lunch! Fire that hibachi up!"

As the sun began to slowly sink, I felt more and more the weight of the world lifting from my shoulders. Knowing the time frame was dwindling, with nothing else to do but wait, praying Popodopoulis came back empty-handed from the hunt, I amused myself writing.

～～～

Summers end, tears fall, hearts mend. Never forget the summer of '65. Can't! Never forget Rosie. Can't! You see, Rosie loved Neil Diamond. I mean the woman loved Neil Diamond! Every album; Neil! Every eight track; Neil! When I was making love to Rosie, I know Rosie was making love to Neil! Once, during 'Cracklin' Rosie', Rosie had her one and only UFO; Unforgettable Female Organism! She screamed out, "NEIL! NEIL!" I did!

There, splayed out before me, lay my answer! My life! My destiny! Yes, at that moment, I decided to become a 'Grand Canyon Ranger'!

～～～

"Anything good?" asked Ari.

"No. Bunch of silly ideas. What's his story, anyway?"

"Who? Pop?" I nodded. "Nothing really. A perv, wealthy, but a wealthy, harmless perv. I don't think he's gotten lucky a day in his life. And, I'd say from the way it's going today, he . . . uh-oh, he's back. I guess we'll find out just how lucky he is." Ari ran off to Popoodoo . . . the car.

There was a brief conversation then, dramatically, Popo crushed the gas, fishtailing out of the parking area unfulfilled . . . again!

～～～

I'll tell you ladies something; he may forget your birthday, may forget your anniversary, he may even forget where he left the kids . . . BUT . . . he will never ever forget the first time Wally came eye-to-eye to the beaver!

~~~

Ari walked back. "Well, I have good news and bad news. Which would you like first?"

"Surprise me."

"Okay, the good news is there's no shoot."

"Aw-w," I feigned a joyful groan.

"The bad news is he ran out of checks."

"What?!?" I blurted, now convinced the idea of money for nothing was too good to be true.

"So, I hope this will do!" Ari beamed from ear to ear, tossing me a wad of cash. He picked up the notebook, scanning my bits as I counted.

~~~

No, I'll never forget ol' Rosie. Now wherever, whenever I hear Neil sing, I think of Rosie . . . I get a budgie!

We bid our adieus. Rosie smiled, and for the last time, Poli-Grip oozed from her upper plate.

You know, it's funny but true; you never forget your first . . . Poli-Girl!

~~~

'Four hundred dollars . . . cash!' "That's it? I mean . . . that's it?" I was happy, not to mention dumbfounded and flabbergasted, but happy at the turn of events.

"That's all she wrote." Ari extended his hand, asking, "You've never been around this porn stuff either, have you?"

"I . . . no."

"Kinda thought so." He tossed the notebook in my lap. "I'm going to pay everyone, grab the kielbasa, and get out of here. Nice working with you." He laughed as he went inside.

I tore out the pages, stuffing them in my pocket along with the bills.

'Oh, you are good at spinning those little miracles now, aren't you?'

~~~

That was it. Like Ripley's, you can Believe It or Not! No porn film was ever shot. My arse was never seen one hundred times it's size on the silver screen. The question I amuse myself with as the years roll by is, of course, had the day gone as expected . . . would I have? My answers vary depending on my frame of mind.

In other words, there are times . . . *I think* . . . I would have done what each of you are thinking.

Yes, even what *you're* thinking!

~~~

Hearing my litany of events, finished reading the bits, Jodi's head slightly shook; a twisted dubious look vied for face time against a credulous smile. "So, that's it?"

"Pretty much. If it wasn't for the money . . . pretty weird, huh?"

Unsuspecting, she threw her arms around me. I recoiled, wincing in pain. "Really burns, huh?"

"Of course it burns!" I yelped. "Do you think I made it up?"

Convinced my non-film debut went as told, her concern turned to the bits. "Is this the only copy you have?" I nodded. "You're sure this is your *only* copy?"

"Yes, but I can make you one. Huh? Little seed money, small film? Watch out Sly Stallone!"

Jodi leaned in, setting a gentle kiss on the one area not on fire. "Why don't we go upstairs? I have some lotion that will make you feel better."

'tic'

'flit'

~~~

We drifted off, smiling, secretly sighing at the non-events of the day. Both wrapped secure in the warmth, care, love, and trust of each other.

~~~

The next day, after much searching, I found my porn script where Jodi had accidentally dropped it.

In the trash.

~10~

'Kind of Quirky'

Two weeks down, two to go 'til New York.

Time together had become tight and pretty scarce. I no longer looked for full make-up stage time; Jodi's schedule would not permit it. Even while doing the 'guitar case' shows, I kept the idea, the 'look' of what I would present at the Biltmore in mind, satisfied, but mentally finessing, tweaking 'The Old Man' both for verbal and visual impact.

More and more, I was bothered with the thought of being a twosome for the past six weeks or so, but always going in different directions. Then, when we did find some time, we never went anywhere, did anything, unless it was 'show' related. Jodi never complained; I know it bothered me more. I kept in mind, once New York was over, whatever may happen, I'd have plenty of time to make it up to her.

~~~

"I have someone I want you to see," Jodi said, all excited, bounding up the bedroom stairs.

"See? Who?"

"Can you write a review?"

"I've written porn, mini-theatre, and bad poetry," I said, half-crowing.

"Good. Now, can you write a review?"

"Of?"

"A stage show."

"Like community theatre?"

"No. My mechanic friend has a friend, who has a friend, who owns a weekly newspaper; they're looking for someone to fill-in for the regular reviewer, who's on maternity leave."

"What does it pay?"

"Nothing."

"Terrific!" My 'thumbs-up' dripped animated sarcasm.

"But—"

"Should I lay down for this?"

"You do get two free tickets to the show."

"Great! That'll fill the tank!"

"There's a few of them coming up, but I want you to see Newley . . . Anthony Newley. You heard of him?"

"I think . . . isn't he British? A singer?"

"Yes, but he's different. Kind of quirky."

"Quirky. Uh-huh. What do you mean 'quirky'?"

"Well, he has a certain . . . he's different. He has a quirky style."

"Who else do I have to choose from?"

She held my look, saying, "Nobody."

"But you just said—"

"I think you should. I want you to see him."

"Why?"

"Because what you're writing, what you're doing in New York is, well, quirky too . . . but in a different way."

"I see. First I'm different, now I'm quirky." I stared at the ceiling, a pondering scowl.

"But in a good way."

"Well, as they say, 'If you've got to be quirky, be good 'n quirky'."

"Who says that? Oh, you! I get it. So, will you?"

"You want me to review . . . for free . . . a quirky Brit. Is that what I'm hearing?"

"At the Music Hall in Boston. Yes!"

Her response so matter-of-fact, the only thing I could say, I said. "For nothing?" She squinted her eyes, pursed her lips. "Okay."

"Really? You're sure?"

"You're the only one who has an inkling of what New York is all about, of what it is I'm doing . . . *whatever* it is I'm doing! You've a reason for this, don't you?" Jodi blushed. "I trust you." Then, she dove on the bed. Seeing Jodi's spirits this high was payment enough.

Leaning over, as I kissed her cheek, she said, "You know . . ." *her chin*, "this will be our very first . . ." *her neck*, "official date . . ." *her shoulder*, "and, we're going to . . ." *her chest*, "Boston to . . ." *her breast*, "the Music Hall . . ." *her nipp . . .*"for *FREE*!" Playfully, she flipped over, plopping on top. Dropping a quick kiss, ala Mae West, she said, "Whatcha got to say 'bout that, big boy?"

I smiled, whispering, "You wouldn't happen to know if my porn script got thrown out with the trash, would you? I haven't seen it for weeks."

"Trash? Really? I have no idea."

'tic'

'flit'

~~~

A week later, with four more open mic nights under my belt, I felt pretty confident about New York. Driving into Boston, heading for the Music Hall to see this Newley fellow, Jodi beside me, the thought, *'Quirky . . . quirky's good,'* crossed my mind, causing me a quiet laugh, or so I thought.

"Penny for your thoughts."

"A penny?!?" I spouted, feigning insult. Then in my best British roll of the tongue, "My good woman, I assure you, my thoughts are worth more than a bloody penny!"

"Oo . . . excuse me your Highness."

"Duke'll do. Ever been to England? No? Me neither. I've always wanted to though, but not like on a quickie vacation. I mean, I've always felt connected with it, the country, somehow. You know? Like I belong; like I should have been born there. You ever feel things weren't like . . . you know?"

"Like I didn't fit?"

"Like . . . exactly!" Light moments with Jodi needn't be funny, silly would do just fine.

Though simple, "No," it was the single note flatness, without the follow-up chit-chat I'd become used to, that caught me off guard.

Letting it slide, I forged on. "Oh. Where would you like to be? To go?"

"I like being here."

"Well, New England's nice, but there's so much more."

"No, I like now. Being here . . . this time . . . this moment." She set her head back on the rest, turning slightly to face me.

"Everything okay?"

"I'm fine." Catching quick glances from on-coming headlights . . ."Really, I am." I saw sadness behind a masked smile. "Tell me a joke."

"No. Something's not . . . what's on your mind?" She was so quiet, pensive. "You can tell me." I'd not seen her like this. "Please."

"Tell me a joke," she repeated.

"If I do, will you—"

"Just tell—"

"Okay, here's an idea; Confessionals . . . for the Hearing Impaired! Whattya think?" Nothing. *That's not particularly funny, but considering she's gone into hysterics over much less . . . *' Now I began to worry. "Did you hear the Catholic Church had thought about marketing their own line of condoms? But, who'd want to buy a 'holey' condom?" Whatever was on Jodi's mind weighed a ton, as she barely smiled. "That's it? For spur of the moment, I thought those were pretty good!" Her smile barely broke.

"You're going away."

"Yes, and you're going with me."

"Just for a long week-end."

"Yeah, then we'll come home."

"No, I'll come home."

"I'll still have the Post Office."

"No," she softly said. "Once you see New York," she turned her head away, gazing out the window. "It's like a melting pot full of idea people, creative people, looking for a shot . . ." She paused, then trailed off, " . . . just a shot."

"I'll have a better shot if you're with me."

It's not like Jodi was not listening, more not hearing me. "I read," she continued, "there's an idea for a new show with an all comedy skit format, looking for writers, quirky writers, that might air late on Saturday nights live . . . Live!"

"What's it called?"

"I don't know, but New York's where you should be, you'll see."

"The only thing that could possibly happen to make me go back, is if I won the scholarship, I couldn't afford it otherwise. Look in the back seat . . . my notebook. Okay, turn to the last page. From what I understand, from what I was told, each of the three groups will have their first elimination round Saturday afternoon. Then, turn back a page, look; on Sunday morning a final elimination. From Thursday to Saturday night, add it up, five rehearsals, five chances to be seen. I figure thirty, forty entries per group to start. That's—"

"A lot of money!" She laughed, though scowling.

"Yeah, it's a money machine. Let's not get into that."

"So, one hundred twenty?"

"Uh-huh, they only need thirty."

"Thirty?"

"Acts . . . for Sunday night's Finals. Quick; thirty acts, three minutes each, one minute between each, add some miscellaneous minutes, that's well over two hours right there! Ninety people . . . acts . . . won't see Sunday night. I'd say my chances are pretty slim."

"Sometimes quirky upsets the flow of things. Your chances are just as—"

"I'm a writer, pretending to be an actor, because I can't find anybody to act out what I've written!" I scowled in thought. "Which, in the long run, is better than being an actor, pretending to be a writer, who can't write out his own act." I trailed off, wondering where to put more commas in what I'd just said. "Did that make any sense at all?"

"No." She finally laughed. "Even if you don't win, you'll have reason to go back."

"What reason?"

"That's just it, it really doesn't matter. You'll find one. Or make one."

"If you're not with me there'll be no reason to stay or go back. What would be the point? Don't you get it? Remember the rocks, the night on the beach? Boulder Isle? I knew then . . . you do all . . . I haven't . . . want to know something?"

"What?"

Glancing back and forth, from watching the road to looking at her, I started. "I'm not used to . . . at the risk of sounding like . . ." *Easy. Now is not the time to get silly or stupid. Take a deep breath. In. Out. Okay. Now.'* "I don't want to be where, anywhere, you're not." *'Breathe.'* "Don't you know I love—"

"Yes."

"Isn't that enough?"

"Yes." She sniffled.

"Then what's—"

"For me."

~~~

The last ovation rose and fell in time with the final curtain. The houselights came up; the audience jostled and milled, making their way up the aisles. My review notes in hand, Jodi asked, "Well, what did you think?"

"Quirky, isn't he?" Jodi laughed. "You're right. I see, or saw . . . see-saw . . . never mind. Okay, you want to know what I think? I would never have come to see this guy. This was . . . this is one more reason why I could never let you go."

With my finger, I underscored notes from the review. 'With the flick of a wrist, the twitch of a finger . . . ' 'Modern day Charlie Chaplin . . . ' 'Storied interpreter . . . ' '(song title) 'Man Who Makes You Laugh . . . ' 'Part pantomime performer . . . ' and on down the page. Then in small block letters at the bottom, I pointed, reading 'note to self'; "It'll Work!" I smiled. "And so will we. I know why you wanted me to see him. You're the only one who knows me, the only one who ever really tried. Quirky *is* good . . . isn't it?"

Her eyes narrowed, nose crinkled, chin wrinkled. 'tic-tic-tic' For a moment we were 'that' couple, 'that' spectacle. Anyone sensitive to public decency should've whispered, 'psst . . . why don't you two get a room somewhere!'

~~~

We exited from the Music Hall into a heavy downpour. Holding hands, laughing like junior high schoolers, we ran the length of the rain slick sidewalk, through the parking lot, to her clown car. All apprehension I'd had earlier, concerning Jodi's state of mind, of her and I, had vanished.

I thought how I had immensely enjoyed Mr. Newley's stylings. Maybe there were others like him, maybe better, it didn't matter. I felt this was not so much about his voice or 'who' he was, more 'what' I had just seen on stage.

Jodi had done, by just believing, by just being, well, Jodi, what no other person, be it lover or friend, had ever done. She accepted, deemed without reservation, to the point of leading me by the hand, showing me how ideas, even my ideas of staging, were worth the time taken to create.

For the first time in memory, way before the night at the Golden Rooster, during the pencil sharpening, scribble pad period, I was awash with optimism, buoyant, dare say . . . fearless . . . now chomping at the bit thinking about New York. Nothing, not a thing, could cause me to falter, to stall now.

Nothing that is, but the sight of keys dangling in the ignition, doors locked, windows rolled up tight!

'Hey, you up there? Why is it I live with this notion I'm nothing more than a thorn in your side? Does the sum total of my existence amount to nothing more than a personal vendetta?'

Once silent prayers on Jodi's part, and loud banging to bust a window open on my part were exhausted, the only late night idea came from Jodi. "I'll call Warren."

"Who?"

"My mechanic."

"You're not going to get a mechanic to come out at this hour!" Once her mind was made up . . . She started walking in the pouring rain. "Where you going?" I shouted, standing under an awning. "This isn't a mechanical problem."

"He has a spare set of my keys."

"Why would he have keys to your car?"

"I told you . . . he's my mechanic."

"So! My mechanic doesn't have keys to my car."

"No, your mechanic has your whole car!"

"Har-har, excuse me if I fail to laugh!" I had to laugh. Even when she was cranky, I thought she was funny.

"Walk with me," she said, rain tears streaking her face.

"We're going to catch pneumonia!" I tried reasoning, but looking in those eyes, at her drenched 'at a loss' expression, I could only say, "Alright, what do we do?"

"Well, unless that's a payphone in your pocket—"

"No, I'm just happy to be here with you! What I meant . . . what direction?"

"I don't know. There," she pointed. I looked . . . nothing; the storefronts were dark, the main streets, except for an occasional Yellow Cab, were deserted. But for the downpour, splatting streetlamp lit puddles, and rushing, gushing, gutter rivulets, it seemed we were the only life in downtown Boston.

Soaked to the bone in search of a phone, we walked, and walked, and ran, and roamed, only to end up in Boston's infamous Combat Zone. Not for the fragile or faint of heart, the Combat Zone is a filthy, sleazy, crime-ridden, four city block slice, crawling with pimps, prostitutes, derelicts, drunks and druggies.

Chock full with nude dance clubs, adult theaters, bars, and porn shops; if the devil built a playground . . . the Combat Zone was it! To further thumbnail a description, imagine a zoo; Boston's finest boys in blue the keepers, but on this rain-drenched night, the keepers are nowhere in sight. The cages have been sprung and mortals scorned by Faith, snubbed of Hope, resigned to Charity, creatures Noah would have spurned . . . freely roam and prowl.

Everywhere . . . printed, plastered, painted, flashing in blazing red neon . . . 'Sex, Sex, Sex' . . . while businesses using 'Pussycat' in their logos were as popular.

Hoping to use the phone, we ducked into the open entrance of the Pussycat movie theatre, yards away from the Pussycat Lounge, across from the Pussycat Puss . . . whatever. Entering the lobby, I felt like we'd stepped into a socially decadent time warp! We stood wordless, surrounded by degenerate posters of films past, playing, and 'coming soon to a theatre near you'; 'The Dear Hummer!' 'The Good Buy Girl!' 'Debby Does . . . Everybody!'

Jodi whispered, "There but for the grace of God go—"

"I!" *'Had I really come this close?'*

With every step, our shoes stuck to the carpet, or what once was carpet. A sign in the ticket booth window read, 'Back in ten minutes'.

"Don't touch anything!" Jodi warned, an uneasy giggle in her voice.

Standing there, we didn't know whether to laugh, run, or run away laughing! Had it not been for the downpour, I know we would have done the latter. My curiosity getting the best of me, "Want to take a peek?" I asked, sounding like a little kid mustering the courage to catch a glimpse of Santa.

I thought about Jodi being offended by what I asked, as I cracked open the double-door. At first, I was *peeking* in. Then, a little wider, so I could *peer* in. It was here when, finding myself holding the door wide open, so I could *gawk* in, Jodi snuck up and *shoved* me in!

We stood at a half wall, behind an audience of about thirty heads. The entire on screen dialogue consisted of long, lingering, sensuous 'ooooohs' and 'ahhhhhs', while grunts and groans from the audience stood out like a velvet Elvis among a show of Monets!

The on-screen close-up was *so* close we weren't sure *what* we were looking at, let alone be it male or female!

Jodi and I looked at each other befuddled, scowling, our lips pursed, mouths tightly closed. In my head, I heard our imminent explosive laughter, saw the projectionist *jump* in fright, stopping the film, which in turn caused a mob scene and, of course, premature evacuation!

"What's that noise?" Jodi whispered.

"Rain? Must be leaks in the roof. Sounds like drops splatt—"

"Eeeew!" We ducked behind the wall, slipped and slid our way out, back to the lobby. "Please tell me that was an extra butter popcorn spill!"

From the ticket booth came a male voice, "Whatever makes you happy, deary!" We turned to find a tiny, old, bald black man, smiling away like Stevie Wonder, but with no teeth. The dam of built-up laughter burst!

Jodi's infectious, embarrassed giggling, the old man's raspy, wheezy, comical laugh, toothless to boot, and my struggles for life's very breath, made eye contact between any of the three of us out of the question!

Repeated attempts requesting use of a phone proved fruitless!

Jodi and I tried everything in the book to gain composure, only to be thwarted, again and again, by the old man's hilarious gum-smacking racket! Not until one of Boston's finest came strolling into the lobby did any sense of normalcy set in.

He was quite large and, given his red-face, I immediately assumed, right or wrong, he was your classic Irish Boston cop. He stood there, shining under the lobby lights. Rain beads fell from his plastic covered hat, rolling down the length, over the girth of his sparkling blue rain slicker. A ring of mini-puddles formed on the filthy threadbare carpet around him. Judging from his smile, despite the beat he had to walk, I thought him to be a man of good disposition.

For a moment, we went silent. Then, "Sightseeing?" said the cop. Blunt as he was, his point was immediately understood; we didn't belong there.

"Our car . . ." I went on to explain. "A phone—"

"A quick local call, please?" Jodi asked, a small plea in her voice.

"Why didn't you say so five minutes ago?" said the tiny ticket booth man, taking a phone from underneath, setting it on the counter.

"We couldn't even *talk* five minutes ago!" We laughed, Jodi dialed.

"Warren? Jodi."

"I'm curious," I said to the little man.

"Boston." Jodi went on, "Keys—"

"I have some porn ideas."

"Locked. Music Hall. Please?"

"Who would I call—"

"Not now!"

"Where would I send—"

153

"Thank-you," I heard Jodi say, as she hung-up the phone.

"Why did you say, 'Not now!' to him?"

"I didn't."

"But I heard you say, 'Not—'"

She kicked my foot to 'pay attention', whispering, "That was for you!"

"What?" I asked, loud and stupefied. "I want to know where my porn ideas can be sent!"

"He's kidding, *Officer!*" Jodi's next sly move was a perfectly placed elbow, "He's just kidding!" to my ribs. This was her way of telling me to 'move, leave, get going'! "Yeah, always the kidder." Funny how an elbow in the ribs can translate all that. "Thank-you. Bye."

~~~

As if all the plumbing in Heaven let go; that's the only way to describe how hard the rain was coming down!

Soaked to the bone, we stopped under every eve, awning, and overhang, seeking refuge from the storm. At each and every stop, Jodi gave me hell for mentioning 'writer of porn' in front of the cop.

"It's just not right! It's like telling him you have ideas for a murder and asking him for suggestions!"

"I don't see what one has to do with the other. You think cops don't watch porn?"

"Yes, but you don't strike up a conversation about it!"

"I wasn't talking to him! I was talking to Stevie Wonders toothless brother!"

And that's the way it went; duck and argue, duck and argue, running around the streets of downtown Boston. We scrambled like drowning rats, from the finest storefronts, through the sleaziest alleys.

All good spirit, found earlier in the evening, pretty much washed away.

Jodi wasn't so much angry at me, we weren't even all that mad at each other, just drenched, exhausted, and annoyed. It felt like it took three times longer to get back. I knew for a fact it had taken that long when we rounded the corner, and there waiting for us, a small blue tow truck. Jodi's clown car door was wide open, a short, pudgy, bespectacled figure, clean, but in work clothes, stood aside it.

Jodi approached him, a few steps ahead of me. They had a quick exchange of words, and she slid behind the wheel. "Warren will drop you at home," was all Jodi said, as she sped . . . putted off.

"Warren? Hi," I said, extending my hand. "I'm Fr—"

"I know. Get in."

~11~

Tic, Talk, Tic, Talk, Tic

9:15 am
my phone

Trying to maintain some sense of calm demeanor, I asked Jodi, "What the hell was that all about?

No, I had a good night. Little weird at the end though, don't you think? Mad? Mad? I do . . . I understand. Alright, it would've been nice if you gave me a clue, some sort of a warning.

Warren? No, he was fine, odd, but fine. Uh, different. Well, if anyone has the 'peculiar look' market cornered, it's him. Don't get me wrong, I'm sure he's a good guy and all, he just had this . . . I don't know. No matter what I said, he'd look at me funny.

Like how? Like a shit-eating grin, is how. I don't know how else to put it.

I know it was storming, yes, it was late. Believe me, I think it was a very big-hearted thing for him to do . . . I do . . . considering he's *just* your mechanic. Which brings up an interesting question; which of us is the bigger dim-wit?

No, not Warren or me! You or me?

Whattya mean 'what do I mean'? You put me in an awkward situation with your *'friend'* and you have to ask? The guy likes you is why. He most certainly does! Sure he do . . . does.

What? What'd he say? Let's see. I said, "Hi. I'm . . ." He said, I hope I remember it all, 'I know. Get in!' Other than an occasional grunt, that was about it, word-for-word. How is it he knew about me at all?

Uh-huh. Oh, *he's* the friend, who has a friend, who has a friend. Well, all I know, his shit-eating grin lasted a lot longer when you were part of the conversation.

Well, being the conversationalist he's not, I'm thinking it's a pretty good bet I was the one who brought you up.

I what? I *sound* funny? What do you mean I *sound* funny? Liberace *sounds* funny! How? Jealous? Of him? Don't be silly! He's your mechanic. And besides, he's way too short for you. I am not! I'm fine.

Uh-huh. Well, yeah, but I don't know too many mechanics that'd do it for a set of keys. I take that back. I don't know *one* mechanic that'd do it for a set of keys!

Uh-huh.

Oh, he's a friend. Like a dating . . . I'm fine . . . like a dating friend? I'm not! I'm asking.

Uh-huh.

Well, you never said that. So, you have dated? High school . . . uh-huh. That was what? Seven, eight years ago? Just him? Uh-huh. Well, no, but knowing you, I find it hard to believe he'd be the only guy you would ever . . . he was the only one who asked you? Oh. I just don't see the attraction. No, not him to you, you to him. Mainly? He didn't seem to have a lot of get up and go; no energy, no spark. I don't know what I mean! Go ahead, laugh! He needs an enema is what he needs! A life enema! You're more like a time-released firecracker.

I've no idea; just made it up.

Uh-huh. No, it hit me on the ride home; it's late, it's storming. There had to be more to him than 'Warren, my mechanic'.

Six years? Uh-huh. That's a long time to date someone. So now he's what? 'My friend, Warren, the mechanical one?' Sure, yes . . . no, I'm fine. Of course. Just a joke . . . little joke.

Jodi, listen, like you said, he's a friend. You have male friends I have female . . . what? Of course I remember the list. I know you were the only name on it! I wrote the damn thing! Are we having our first fight? I can't tell.

Breathe. Again. Deeper. Deeper. Deep . . . you okay? Really? I would of passed out by now!

It's good to hear your laugh.

So, are we still on for New York? Six more days. Just checking. I confirmed the room reservations . . . are you kidding? That's all I can think of. I'm looking at a brochure of the hotel . . . the Biltmore. It's a nice old building, near Central Park, steps from Broadway. What's playing? I don't know! I don't get there often, well, ever. Is it? You can be my tour guide.

The main room looks like it seats at least a thousand. It's hard to . . . it has a balcony! You're not going to believe . . . Jodi, this is a theatre! No, I mean a real theatre! "ey, Juliet. S'me, Romeo. S'up?' Yeah, really. Fancy schmancy!

You know what just occurred to me? *'What the hell have I done?'* How's that for confidence? Stop laughing! It's not funny . . . well, maybe a little. I feel like something is going to happen. Do you feel that?

Uh-huh. No, it's not going to be a New York audience. I think it's going to be a cross-section of people, mostly parents, from all those neighborhood hole-in-the-walls up and down the East coast. A lot of them thinking their kid is the ticket. You know what I want to see?

Uh, well, the Statue of Liberty? No, well yeah, before we leave, but what I really want to see? All of the other acts; the adults. I want to see what I'm going up against. Well, first off, they'll be weeded out and, think about it, these aren't kids with someone bankrolling their way. These are adults convinced whatever it is they have will change their lives. They're paying their own way, so they have to believe they have . . . whatever it is you have to believe you have.

Do I believe I have 'it'? It? I'm still not sure what I have. A cutting from a play that doesn't exist? An excerpt from a book not yet written? I don't know. All I know is it's original. I'd like to think a voting panel of New York notoriety would take note of that. Right . . . this time the panel selects.

As far as my part, most times it works, sometimes not, that's scary enough. Now there's a panel, that's even scarier, you never know. Writing first,presentation, then acting. This is New York. I want to write. I have to think this is right up their alley.

Well, if you wrote comedy, it would be very unprofessional to be judged by a panel of sci-fi, poets, and gumshoe writers. Me? I'd rather entertain ten thousand open-minded readers than a panel with a personal agenda. I mean, no matter how good they are, they don't know where you're coming from. One thing's for sure, they will react, somehow. And, that's about all I know.

Well, I know that too. Right back at you.

Uh-huh. No, at you.

Uh-huh. No, at you.

Uh, Jodi, hold on just a minute."

~~~

Opening the tableside window, "Hi. Yeah, nice day. Do me a favor? Could you tell the boy not to point his BB gun this way? Thanks; accidents happen. What? You told him he has to skin and eat anything he shoots! Well, there you go. If he shot me, I'd be screwed . . . twice! Look, a squirrel! That's dinner *and* a hat!"

~~~

"Jodi? Hi. Nothing. Poachers . . . never mind. Tonight? Tonight, I'm doing a church basement in town. No, witty one, not painting and papering! It's like a coffeehouse, but nicer. I don't know. There's something special, almost spiritual, about church basements. Can I get any more redundant? Could be just the acoustics; they all seem to have great acoustics.

Dinner? Tonight? You did? When? I'm sure I mentioned this show to you at some time. If you'd rather not, I'll be okay. No, no make-up is okay. I'll just do the story. I want to do something like last night again. Okay, a date, but with a better ending. Oh, well, whenever you can free up . . . right, four days in New York. Rick just drove in, he's taking me to pick up my car. Talk later.

What did you say? Liver? Did you say 'liver'? Yes you did. 'See you later, liver,' that's what it sounded like to me. Subconsciously, you think of me as a slab of meat, don't you? No, that's fine. Lover, liver, spleen, kidney, femur; I don't care. Just make a little room for me in there somewhere. I gotta go. Me, too. Me, too. I do. Rick's standing right here. You are. Of course you are. Bye."

Hazy eyed in his finger rolled fog, "She is what?" Rick asked.

"My liver. Don't ask. Your head'll explode."

~~~

10:05 am

Out the door, walking to his car, I asked, "Mind if I drive?" Rick's buzzed state had me concerned we would not make it to Boston for a day or two.

"I'm capable," he challenged, focusing through a major case of red-eye.

"But I know right where we're going."

"So do I."

"Where we going?"

"The garage."

"What garage?"

"You tell me."

"I thought you knew."

"I forgot."

"I never told you."

"Well, if you're gonna be that way, you drive!" Stoned, the guy's a walking skit.

~~~

10:12 am

"How much they getting you for?" he asked, as I pulled into traffic.

"Repairs? Four hundred and change."

"Cash?"

"No, buffalo hides. What're you smoking there? The really dumb stuff?"

"Work must be going well."

"I was in a porn film. Made four hundred dollars." *'No I wasn't! Yes I did!'*

Rick looked at me in a grinning stupor. "You wish!" He laughed; I laughed.

'He'll never know.'

~~~

10:16 am

"You must be getting your forty by now. Any overtime?"

"You want the job?"

"There's a lot worse. You don't talk about it much."

"Try not to think about it much."

"Still goin' to New York?"

"That's the plan. Leave Thursday morning . . . return Monday. Then, with a little bit of luck, quit Tuesday."

"You would, wouldn't you?"

"In a heartbeat."

"Suppose nothing comes of this. What then?"

"Life goes on."

"Would you still quit?"

"Neither rain, snow, sleet, etcetera, etcetera. The mail must get through!" Though making light of the adage, I gripped the steering wheel, cringing at the thought.

~~~

10:19 am

"You've got a good thing staring you right in the face and you can't see it."

"I see Jodi, New York, and the job. In that order."

"That's whacked."

"Ever heard of a religion where the belief is you get to live your life over, again and again?" Rick stared with an all too familiar grin. "And, with each rebirth, you come closer to realizing what your being, your true core essence, is all about?"

"You're going to be a monk?"

"Ha-ha . . . no. Look, maybe I'm kidding myself, but until New York is over, I'd like to think there's more to *all this* than junk mail and postal punchlines."

"What about Jodi?"

'What about Jodi?' "Up until the night of the first show, then later, when I really got to know her, 'til then . . . I couldn't get lucky if I was a warden in a women's prison with a fistful of pardons!" Rick choked on a toke. "And another buck goes up in smoke," I noted, a chuckle in my sigh of his waste.

Through his choking, "What?" he finally blurted.

"Old joke. You know what I mean."

"What I meant was . . . would she go with you to New York?"

"She's going."

"To the show, but would she move there?"

"No. Yes. I don't know! That's what's throwing a wrench in everything."

"It's only been a couple months. Maybe she thinks you're rushing it. Maybe there's somebody else."

"What? No. Why would you say that? She has her friends, a job she loves, her family lives near. I can't expect her to chuck everything, go running off on some wild goose chase of mine. She has a life, responsibilities."

~~~

10:24 am

"Want to get a burger?" Lost in thought, "I've got a . . ." I sped past the burger joint. "coupon. Two for one," he mumbled. "What's buggin' you?"

"What? Nothing. Okay, it's like the closer New York gets, the more distant I feel she gets."

"Maybe she's seeing somebody."

"What the . . . what're you? A friggen broken record?"

"Don't jump down my throat! I saw her with some . . . well, I didn't see him."

"Him? Him who?"

"About a week, week and a half back, Shirley saw Jodi with some guy."

"I know all about him. That's Warren, an old boyfriend, well, if you want to call him that. He's a mechanic, an old friend."

"No."

"Yes."

"No."

"What?"

"This guy was a cop."

~~~

10:**
time stopped

'I really don't need this!' The barrage of what, where, and whens I rained on Rick while speeding down the highway, followed by a white-knuckle game of emotionally driven 'dodge 'em' with downtown Boston traffic, "Up yours, buddy! Oh, yeah? Right here! Right here!" had Rick one move away from grabbing the door handle, exiting the thrill mobile! All I received in return, from my vapid cross-exam, was a severe case of the 'I don't knows'.

Between work, Jodi, and three, four, sometimes five nights a week, chasing stage time wherever, whenever, preparing for New York, my plate was full. I neither wanted, needed, nor had room for surprise leftovers. No matter how I juggled them in my mind, any combination of two worked fine. Soon, very soon, one of the three would have to go.

Dropping the entire New York idea was not out of the question. Though I'd drive myself crazy needing to know 'what if', it wasn't a matter of life or death. And, despite how disheartened, nay loathsome I'd become of the Post Office, in case New York fizzled, fact's a fact, I needed the job. Although the thought of thirty years, *thirty years*, of not matching one customers face to a Wanted Poster, then retiring, in complete and total denial of severe advanced senility . . . rested very heavy on my mind. *'How would I know? As long as I'm not drooling, the neighbors will just think I'm eccentric!'* And I wanted Jodi.

Two 'needs' and a 'want'.

'Needs first, your wants will have to wait,' rang clear as a bell.

~~~

10:42 am

"Thanks for the ride."

"No problem."

"You sure?"

"Yeah."

"Let go of the handle."

~~~

11:45 am
Jodi's phone

"Hello? Hi. Did you get your car? What's the matter? Who? Shirley? Oh, your bedside bimbo. I remember. She saw me with a guy? A cop? And you believe her? No, I'm asking you. You believe her, don't you? No, you answer me. You do?"

(click)

~~~

11:47 am

"Hello? That's for me to know and for you to find out!"

(click)

~~~

11:48 am

"Yes? No kidding! Did I say I wasn't? Did I? Yes, yes, okay. It was me! My brother! Are you happy now? Good! Listen, I've something else to make your day . . . screw New York!"

(click)

~~~

11:50 am

(click)

~~~

11:50 am

(click)

~~~

11:50 am

(click)

~~~

11:51 am
my phone

"Jodi, do not hang-up on me again! Promise? Give me your wor . . ."

(click)

~~~

9:39 pm

"Jodi, look . . . you tell me he's your brother, of course I believe you."
'I want to!' "Why wouldn't I? We've not lied to each other to this
point, have we?" *'Yes? No? Yes?'* "No, I don't think Shirley meant any
harm." *'Or did she?'*

What? Oh, tonight's show, I couldn't go. I mean I could . . ." *'And
I did, then raced home, hoping you'd call.'* "but I just wanted some
time alone to think.

About? Well, if you're not going to New York, why should I? Because,
you wanted to be part of it . . . you're part of it. What are you . . .
oh, don't get all worked up. We're fine. Believe me.

New York's right around the corner. I feel good about the material.
My girlfriend has a cop for a brother, and Raymond can't touch me!
All's right in the world . . . who was that? I heard a voice . . . there
it is again. Do you have company? Little late isn't it? Anyone I . . .
your brother.

Uh-huh.

What's he want? A towel?

Sure, I'll hold.

10:05 pm

10:08 pm

10:14 pm

A *funny* plumbing problem? Talk to you tomor . . ."

(click)

~~~

169

10:15 pm

10:16 pm

10:17 pm

10:18 pm

"Hello, Shirley?"

~12~

'A Comfortable Piece'

9:04 am
next morning

'ring' I startled at the kitchen phone, jumped from bed, fumbled with my robe, and on shaky legs, *'ring'* made my way to the stairs; fully anticipating Jodi's call.

Five steps down I hear, *'ring'*, "Hello? This is Jodi. Who? Shirley. Hi." I sat on a stair, cradling my chin in my arms. "He's sleeping. I don't know. Called late? Last night? He mistook your mother for you?"

All I could do was shake my head.

"Sure, hold on. Go ahead. *'Sorry you missed his call. Will be in all day. Your dad said your mother is taken.'* I'll give him the message. What?

Oh, yes, that was me. Oh, really? I wish I'd seen you. You should've said 'Hi'. We could've had a coffee. Hm? I'll tell him. Bye."

I watched from my perch as Jodi centered the note on the table, picked up what appeared to be a full travel bag, and tiptoed to the backdoor.

"Anything I can do?" I asked, appearing in the kitchen entrance.

"You can call Shirley back."

"Jodi—"

"If she's not in, you could give her mother another thrill."

"Jodi—"

"Or a heart attack!"

"So, you know. I called, but never spoke to her. It's not like she came over."

"No, but if you had, she would have."

"What're you, psychic? A seer of all that never happened? By the way, how's Warren? Your brother? How's your plumbing?"

"Listen to yourself! What's the difference?"

"The difference is I had a weak moment! You seem to have weak . . . weeks!"

"I don't need this!" she choked, grasping the doorknob.

"I don't either!" Jodi threw open the door. Off-balance, she hefted the travel bag to her shoulder, missed, the bag falling to the floor. From an unzipped pocket popped a hairbrush, toothpaste, and assorted items. "Going away for a few days?"

"I was," she said, kneeling, scooping the items back in.

I knelt to help. "Any place special?"

"It was."

"Not anymore?"

"No."

"Why? What's happening? Why's everything falling apart?"

"It's not you, well, it is you . . . no it's not, it's me. Between my job, shows I'm committed to, your shows, New York, *you*, I think I've bit off more than I can chew."

"You know what then?"

"What?"

"Take smaller bites." During this moment of nose blowing, tear wiping, and tittering, we stayed kneeling in position. Finally, "Stay," I said, and the floodgates opened.

~~~

9:26 am

'thwick – zing – ting' My head shot up! *'What in the name of . . . ?'* I can't be held to this, I'm not positive, but I swear I heard, "What're you shootin' at, son?"

"Nothin'," the kid with the BB gun shouted, running to his father.

"We don't shoot at nothin', boy!"

"I thought I saw a beaver."

We pulled ourselves together, moving upstairs, out of view of the open door. *'There's something wrong with that kid. I know there is!'*

~~~

Later that morning.

"Are you sleeping?" I asked.

"Yes."

"Oh."

"Rouse me."

'Arouse?' "Okay, just 'til you're awake."

And . . . I did.

~~~

Early that afternoon.

"Want to—"

"Yes."

And . . . we did.

~~~

Later that afternoon.

"Are you getting up?"

"Yes," I murmured, as Jodi whipped off the comforter.

"No you're . . ." she started, followed by a 'tic' and a giggle. "There we are."

And . . . she did.

~~~

Early that evening.

Sprawled out, exhausted, we lie there, not moving, neither making a sound. Thought-free gazes spoke tender volumes, but not a word was heard. Then, she stretched . . . and took the words right out of my mouth!

And . . . we did.

~~~

Later that evening.

"Where you goi—"

"Food! Water!"

"Oh."

"It can wait."

And, we fell asleep, not knowing who did what, when, last.

~~~

Next morning.

"Would you like—"

I smiled, eyes closed. "You're kidding!"

"Breakfast?"

"Oh."

"What would you enjoy?"

"You . . . on a bagel."

She put on my robe. "Don't get up.'tic' I'll surprise you."

"That I could . . . that'd surprise me!" 'flit' And down the stairs she went.

Calm and content, awash with an all too, as of late, infrequent inner-peace, and best of all aware of it, *It's a beautiful thing,'* I took pad and pen off the nightstand. Jotting, *'. . . calling Jodi's muse . . .* 'at the top of the page, I settled back, settled in.

~~~

Bedside scribblin'
October 28, '75.

'Pull the blinds tight, draw the curtains, dim the light, we're going to stop the hurting, for a while, for tonight. What's it all mean to anyone, let alone you or me? If it's going to make us feel a part of, then who is going to know?'

"Want some music?"

'Who is going to care?'

"How about some Joe Cocker?"

'Who gives a damn, really?'

"Okay."

'So rest weary mind from dusk 'til dawn, for now sweet Princess and I, the Prince, we shall be equal 'til tomorrow, then again, again but pawns. Fools to think we are different for any longer than the time we have for ourselves allowed, for we in time would only fall victim of the crime, of letting our senses, our feelings, run the same as the maddening crowd.'

"But I'm just a soul whose . . . lalalalalalala . . . don't let me be misunderstood!"

'Oh, lay back, lie back, gently, loves motion so slow. Tonight's night won't come again, and time, oh, time, that rascal of a friend of yours

and mine, has placed this night in our path . . . who are we to say, "No, no this night shan't happen."

"Yeaaaah . . . Feelin' alright. I'm not feelin' too good myself . . ."

'Stars shine, stay bright, show my love, my love of tonight, my friend of tomorrow, that darkness offers a blanket of secret innocence. Secrets? Yes, secrets, echoing in the warm summer night's breeze. Echoes of a power, of a passion, of two entwined, rolling, loving, shining as one, finding all which was said not to be, can and is and from now on will be, will be . . . oh yes, love, it will be.'

"Do you need anybody? I need someone to love . . . (cough) waaa (yeck) aaa!"

'Until the morning sun finds us, putting us back in sight. Once more a part of the maddening crowd, that is til the night, oh, the night; sweet, sweet, night.'

"She came in through the bathroom window!" This lyric concluded Jodi's impromptu Joe Cocker songfest sing-along. Handing me a large cup of coffee, "Careful, it's hot," she sat on the bed's edge. "So, when do you write? I need to know so I don't disturb you."

Hearing this in all its innocence, knowing she hadn't a clue, I lost it!

As if spilling, splashing, bathing hot coffee, *by my own hand,* on an exposed Mr. Happy was not ridicule enough, Jodi sat in bug-eyed awe as I wriggled, twisted, jerked about, squealing like a liquored prom queen! Grabbing a handful of tissues off the nightstand, I suffocated Mr. Happy, in hopes of absorbing the burn!

Breathing under control, I looked to Jodi. Misty beads, a spray of Chock Full 'O Nuts, covered her face. She sat statue still, not saying a word, holding my cock-eyed stare. Something about her look told me, *'Whatever you do, 'I'm sorry', won't be enough!'* One of us was going to crack! The 'look' she held was just about to nudge me over the edge when . . . Not breaking our 'look', slowly I lifted the wad of tissues, holding the clump between us. "Mr. Happy would like you to have these."

'flit'

Jodi burst!

'And in first place . . . '

It's the little things.

'Bring on New York!'

~~~

**Early that afternoon
on Boulder Isle.**

"It happens when it happens."

"Then how will I know when to leave you alone?"

"It's not all about being alone," I explained, gazing out over craggy Boulder Isle as far as the eye could see. "I could write right now." I fixed my eyes on infinity, where powder-blue sky met deep-blue ocean, where Heaven and Earth surely meld. "If I had something to write about."

"Oh."

"It's about being comfortable with your surroundings, being at peace with who's near."

"Then my being around for long periods wouldn't distract you?" *'What is she . . . If I didn't know better . . . Is she saying what I'm thnking? Wait! Did I just offend her? I think I did. I did! She's trying to say something and I'm mucking it all up. Fix it!'*

"I didn't say you wouldn't distract me." Jodi smiled. *'Good work!'* "I just don't think you'd be so much a distraction, as you would be a comfortable . . ." *'I don't believe I just said that!'*

"Piece?" I was impressed with how fast it hit her. "I'd be a comfortable *piece!*"

'Why don't you just get the kid with the BB gun back here . . . have him slowly shoot your brains out! Let's say, oh, all night!'

"That's the nicest thing anybody ever said to me!"

"That's the saddest thing I've ever heard!" Her funny bone tickled, feigning a tear, she slid onto my boulder, 'tic', and snuggled. We lay in the sunshine, drifting in and out of a comfortable pie . . . peace.

~~~

Later that afternoon.

"What were you writing earlier?" Jodi asked, curling up on the sofa, as I sat in the recliner.

"Something for you, eventually."

"Eventually? Whose is it now?" she asked, smiling.

"Cute. Mine." Stretching out, I pushed the recliner back. "Right now, it's either poetry with potential, or potentially bad poetry."

"Where is it?"

"When I'm done."

"When'll that be?"

"Soon." I looked over the bridge of my nose. "Why? Going somewhere?" The corners of her mouth turned up ever so slight. I followed her movements as she got up. Stepping over my prone middle, she stood, straddling me.

"Yes, I'm going somewhere." She loomed over me, her hands set top of the chair, one either side of my head. Waiting, anticipating, expecting at any second for the other shoe to drop, I held a chuckle in check. Her face drew closer, closer.

"Oh? Where you going?"

I heard her answer ever so faint, felt the whispered words as they washed over, poured over me, warming my very core. "Right here."

And, much to Mr. Happy's chagrin, we did.

~~~

Early that evening.

'ring' I sat upright. "Jodi," I whispered, "you awake? It's seven o'clock."

'ring' Her face in the pillow, she turned her head just enough to look at me with one eye open. "How do you know?" she whispered back. "Where's the little hand?" *'ring'* "On the seven." Leaning over . . ."Big hands near the twelve." I lightly kissed her neck.

"Oh, good," she mumbled, "he can tell time." She dragged herself up . . . butt first. "I'll put the coffee on."

"In the evening!"

"And," she said, collapsing back down, "another prayer is answered!"

"I say we celebrate!"

"Hear! Hear!" She yawned. "Celebrate what?"

"We made it!"

"What? You didn't think you'd last the weekend? I'm proud of you! I knew you had it in you . . . or, vicey-vercy."

"No," I said, with a playful slap to her butt. "New York is this Thursday. You have the week off! I have the week off! We made it!"

"If I give you a dollar will you smack the other one?"

"No! Up! Up!"

"Two dollars?"

'ring' "Get yourself together, woman! We're going out!"

"Where?"

'ring' "Dinner. County fair. I don't care! Any place your little heart desires."

"Dancing?"

'ring' "No. Sorry, I got carried away."

"Can we please get a phone installed up here?"

'ring' "I will." *'Can we?'* "If you pull yourself together and go out stepping with me."

"Step dancing?"

'ring' "No."

"Damn! So close!"

"C'mon!" *'ring'* I ran downstairs. "Hello. Hello. Hello?" Hanging up, "What would you like to do?" I yelled.

"There's no need to yell. Food would be good. Let's go to Boston, have dinner, walk around the city. Maybe visit our friends in the Combat Zone." Jodi appeared in the kitchen's entrance, rumpled and frumpled, but dressed, her travel bag, her life's possessions, tucked under arm.

"Look at you," I said, smiling at the picture framed in the doorway.

"What?" she said, giving in to a grin. "What?" Her blush ripened rapidly. "What?" She walked toward me. "What?" As she advanced, "What?" not breaking her gait, "What?" she held my look, "What?"

her smile. "What?" Now face to face, "What . . . can I do for you?"

'ring' "Everything."

"Kiss my face!"

"Now, *that* I can do!" *'ring'* "Damn phone!"

"We'll get back to that," she said, scuffling to the bathroom. "I gots to pee!"

'ring' "Jiggle the handle!" I reminded, reaching for the wall phone. *'Gots . . . ?'* "Hello? Hel . . . She is. Yes. Who's this? Oh . . . hold on." Jodi stepped in to the kitchen, smile gone, brow furrowed. "It's for you." Our eyes met for a second . . . a second that took forever to pass. Looking away, I extended the receiver.

No tics.

"Your brother."

No flits.

And, the receiver hit the floor.

~13~

'Eve of Destruction'

Because the rocking chair had to make the trip, the thought of loading up Jodi's car never made it past the talking stage. There was something about the sight of a jam-packed VW clown car, orange to boot, with a wicker rocker tied to the roof, barreling across America's highways, that struck us as odd . . . funny, but odd.

We settled for plan two; pack my car Wednesday night, for an early get-away Thursday morning, and a leisurely Boston to New York drive. Jodi's to-do list included breakfast in Rhode Island, an antique shop or two in Connecticut, lunch at the landmark Broadway Deli, finally registering at the Biltmore by mid-afternoon.

Late Thursday morning, after carefully strapping the rocker to the convertible top, I left, alone, driving straight through to New York.

~~~

Since Jodi left Sunday night, no contact was made by either of us to speak, to explain what was going on. As much as I wanted to see her, talk to her, just wanted her, though I had one hundred questions, I stopped from calling as many times. Before I could bring myself to do anything, at the very least, I felt I was owed an explanation.

Speeding along, I tried convincing myself, *'This was put into motion way before Jodi!'* This is the way it has to be. She just happened to happen. No big whoop. *'But what the hell happened?'* "That's what I'd like to know!"

'Her husband . . . that's what happened!'

"Um, she's not married."

'Her boyfriend!'

"Um, he's a friend."

'Her brother!'

"Um-m, that's illegal!"

'New York! New York! New York! Over and over and over, that's what really happened!' I have to admit even I was past irritated hearing it. As if I didn't already harbor lifelong contempt for the Yankees, now the entire State of New . . . *'Let it go. Let it go.'*

There's nothing worse than a road trip . . . *'There's nothing worse than a road trip . . . alone.'* With no radio! *'Yes there is.'* " . . . pheoo . . . pheeooo . . ." *'Geezus!'* "I can't even whistle!" *'Told you! You rhythmless fuck!'*

My self-destruct pattern of thought could drive a sober man to drink!

"Focus . . . focus." *'Where are you going? What're you doing? This may work, you know. Nothing, nothing that is, short of a committee of narrow-minded elitist bungholes, a cluster of closet twittleheads, can interfere now!'*

"Get a grip!" *'This isn't the Golden Rooster . . . it's the Biltmore . . . New York City! All's fair in blood and strip bars! Maybe I should write a book.'* "A Committee of Bungholes." *'Hm-m.'* "A Cluster of Twittleheads." *'There's a story in there somewhere.'*

Grasping, gasping, for a hint of a chuckle, a speck of light-heartedness, just as a grin crept near, thoughts of Jodi jerked me back.

"I really don't friggin' need this!" I further articulated this melodramatic outburst to the dashboard, adding emphasis with a hearty slam. It would be funny to say the radio suddenly came alive from the blow, playing the Stone's 'Satisfaction' or Barry McGuire's 'Eve of Destruction' . . . but it didn't. "I don't need this!"

'No, but you do need her.'

"What does she want?"

'Isn't it obvious?'

"No! No, it is not obvious!"

'It's as plain as the zit on your face.'

"What is?"

'The zit on your—'

"But she's excited!"

'You're excited!'

"It's the same thing!"

'Oh?'

~~~

185

"Welcome to the Biltmore. Sign here. Your key and itinerary through Monday check-out. Bags? Bellman! Would you take this lugg . . . sorry? Rocking chair? The rooms *are* completely furnished, sir. Oh, the show! Excuse me. You're all set. You're welcome, sir. Good luck. I was just wondering . . . the rocker? I think I may. I do possess a keen imagination, sir. No? Well, maybe I wouldn't then. Yes, fine, some other time perhaps. Enjoy your stay." It's not that he actually said it, not that I really heard it, *'prick',* it was all in his look.

"Excuse me?"

"Enjoy your stay, sir."

~~~

'Itinerary . . . itin . . . ' I collapsed into a three hour napping coma. "Yawwwwn . . ." *'stretch 'n grow, stretch 'n grow'* "Itinerary." **Meet Main Ballroom – Six o'clock.**

"Front desk. Good evening, sir. Yes, the guest with the rocking chair. No problem at all, sir. Time? Six twenty-seven. Yes, about thirty minutes ago in the Main Ballroom. Six twenty-seven. Yes, for a half hour now. I'm positive, sir. The big hand? Sir, I have a number of guests' waiting to check in. Did you receive your itinerary? Yes? Will there be anything else? Enjoy your night." Again, it wasn't that he actually said it, it wasn't that I really heard it, *'prick',* I just sensed it.

"What?"

(click)

~~~

I stood at the rear of the Main Ballroom looking at every act ever conceived since Bo Jangles first stood on a soapbox. *'Let me entertain you . . . '*

Mentally vacant, emotionally destroyed, so far removed from the very reason I was there, I could have kicked a puppy! No, that's not true. I like puppies. I could've slapped the grin off a Hari Krishna though! As my *li'l black dad so often said, 'It's a mighty fine line between a ponytail and a horses ass!'

Sporting a shiny baldhead, photographer's pouched vest, black muscle T, tinted aviator glasses and headset, Commando Techie took center aisle announcing, "The Adult sound checks begin at nine this evening!"

'I wonder what Jodi's doing?'

"The Adult sound checks begin at nine this evening! Make a note."

'I wonder who she's with? Why do I have to think she's with somebody?'

"The Adult sound checks begin at nine this evening! Listen up!"

'I don't care! Yes I do! No, I really don't . . . just come to me . . . come to me when you can. Listen to yourself! You lose it now . . . this is pathetic!'

"The Adult sound checks begin at nine this evening! 'No shows' will be dropped!"

'I've waited so long for this to happen. Can't I have both? This and her kiss?'

"Any questions?"

"What time are the Adult sound checks?" *'He didn't have to put it like that!'*

~~~

10:10 pm

"Number one thirty-four."

The walk to the stage, I swear, was a mile long! To use the term 'ill prepared' is putting it mildly. Disaster loomed; I knew it. My footing heavy, like slogging through quicksand, I made my way to the gallows; Commando Techie my executioner. "Glad you made it."

"Got here fast as I could," I said, with a hereditary smirk. *'Bite your tongue. Hard. Harder!'* "I have a cassette. Here. Background music." *'Oh, my dear sweet Geezus! Now that's a stage!'* "Carry okee? I don't sing . . . never heard of it." *'That is one enormous fuc—'* "Huh? What was it again? Keri-oki? Ah, Japanese." *'Hey up there . . . paying attention? You see what's going on here? You could fit all of Rhode Island up there!'* "What? I don't know. What does it mean?" *'I'm going to fill that vast wasteland?'* "The band didn't show up?" *'I really don't think so!'* "Doesn't sound like something that'd catch on here." *'Oh, was that a joke?'* "What?"

"You might want to get up on stage." *'Oh, I might?'* "I'll be right back," Commando Techie said, turning away.

Ill timed, I asked, "Should I get my rocking chair?"

Throwing the cassette down, "Fook this!" he clearly said.

"What?"

"Look, Sport, I'm at the end of a very long day. I still have four more acts after you, an hour or two of paperwork, a drive home to Queens, and a wife who thinks every night is her wedding night!" *'Did he say 'fook'?'* "Then come seven AM, I get to do it all over again. Am I drawing you a clear enough picture?"

'You're every New York Yankee I ever hated!' "The rocker is part—"

"Part of the reason I'm gonna jack you out of here if you don't get up there!"

Trying to will one last composed nerve ending through my entire body, turning, I walked up the platform, over the footlights. Standing at the microphone on this huge barren stage, I looked out at fifty or sixty varied category performers, techies, and hangers-on, scattered in the seats, on the floor, hanging over the balcony. *'This is not going to work.'* Commando Techie hit the start button.

"Ah, yes, another year past, ah, but what a year it was. Now I look across the tables, see the same old faces, hear the same old fables. Oh . . ." *'Jodi . . .* '

"'ey, Sport . . . yo'kay?" The music stopped. "We're just doin' sound and lights. No pressure. Wanna try that again?"

"Can I sit? This feels awkward. I've never done it standing up." *'Fook you!'*

"Want a rocker?" *'Twice!'*

New Yorker or not, muscles or no muscles, "Look, I've had a long day too! There's a rocking chair involved in what I'm doing, okay? I just didn't know whether to bring it or not!"

"I know," he said, snapping an index card. "I have all your info right here."

"Oh. Well, if you know, what'd you get all mental about?"

"Fifteen hours, Hot Shot. To me you're number one hundred thirty-fookin'-four . . . four more to go. Now, would you like a rocker?"

"No."

The houselights went down; banks of tints and shades came up. A roving spot shot on, clouding my vision, as if I was looking through gauze. The energy in the room stilled. I walked to the lip of the stage and sat. My music came up, and for three minutes, *'Jodi'*, I mumbled, stumbled, and crumbled.

~~~

11:10 am
Friday

"Front Desk? Could I get Room Service, please?" *'One hundred thirty-eight entries . . . three categories.'* "Front desk? No, Room Service. Yes." *'Ten finalists per category . . .* '"What? Front Desk? I'm trying to

189

get Room Service. Fine." *'That means one hundred eight acts will be cut by Sunday morning.'* "Front . . . Look, all I want is a cup of coffee. Well why didn't you say so? No you didn't! Because you didn't ask, that's why! No you did not! Yes, yes, I'll hold! I'll fuc . . ." *'Twenty-six in the Adult Category . . . cut sixteen there.'* "What? There's coffee in the Main Ballroom? I'm not in the Main Ballroom! In my room! When? Ten o'clock! You're kidding! Are there doughnuts? Dough balls? Anything? Just coffee, I see. Thanks. Sorry I . . . What?"

(click)

~~~

11:32 am

Commando Techie stood at the back of the room, spotting me as soon as I entered. "What's on your Christmas list? A fookin' watch?"

"Who's he?" I asked.

"Who?"

"Pretty Boy Floyd over there."

"Not sure. I know he's part of the organization. Promoter, maybe." I scowled. "See the old lady with the fur, the heavy make-up? She's the bank . . . his mommy."

"He looks like a pimp." And, in fact, he did. Mid-thirties, about five foot five, with thin, slick, shiny black hair. The top four buttons of his shirt opened clear to the arc of his potbelly. Dancing across his hairless chest were four gold necklaces, one longer than the other, and a good-size medallion on a heavy silver chain. Three rings decorated his pudgy left hand, four on his right. His jowls wiggled and jiggled in unison with his constant flapping mouth. Girls of all ages hovered around him, giggling, flirting, all a-sparkle trying to glean a morsel, some mystical tidbit, for succeeding in 'the biz'. "Is he on the panel?"

"Why?"

"Well, if he is, I'd like to know so I can stay out of his way. If he's not, after I piss him off, at least I know I still have a shot."

"Why would you piss him off?"

"I don't know. Just seems I've been pissing people off since I arrived. The bellman and the front desk clerk have chosen me Prick of the Week." *I'll be damned! Commando Techie has a sense of humor . . . at my expense of course.'* "Look what happened last night with you and me. In twelve hours, I've managed to piss off three people!"

"This is New York. That's not that bad."

"I slept for eight of them! I'm zero for three in my New York social skills!"

He laughed. "I wouldn't worry about it."

I spotted the urns off to my left, "I need coffee," and stepped toward them.

He followed along, saying, "Maybe today'll be better. Stranger things have happened." *'Is Commando Techie showing a soft spot through that hulking exterior? Okay, I made a new friend. A New York hard ass maybe, but still, a friend's a friend.'*

"It's like their last series," I began, not knowing when to shut-up, "when the Red Sox spanked the Yankees, I mean humiliated them soundly, three out of three. I didn't mean to piss anybody off. I just came here to try to win, like the Red Sox just wanted to win . . . not humiliate the Yankees to the point of serving up their asses on a silver platter the way they did. I think it's a gift."

"Fook you!" He executed a spot-on 'about face' and walked away.

"See!" *'It's a fookin' gift!'*

~~~

191

7:15 pm

The morning run-through was a disaster. *'Here we go again!'*

Up to now, the feel of the competition was to get comfortable, get to know one another. Tonight was the last time to 'feel the stage, find your spot'. Tomorrow, after two full preliminary rounds, morning and afternoon, the first cut happens. *'That'll be a deep one.'* I'm still not sure who's who, but I know people are watching. *'Get it together, will you!'* "What'd Jodi say?" *'Be professional, you never know who's watching.'*

"Excuse me?"

"'Oh, hi. You caught me talking to myself, out loud." She looked at me. "It's okay. Sane people do it too." She giggled. "You part of the show?" She nodded. "I've been to all the run throughs so far, how'd I miss you?" She smiled. "Talk much?" She laughed.

"I'm Bonnie," she said, extending her hand.

"Bonnie. Hi, I'm Fr—"

From over my shoulder, though whispering, "We're waiting on you!" Commando Techie's voice boomed.

"Excuse my friend."

"You got to get up there," he said, leaving no doubt where I should be at that exact moment.

"I'll be right back," I said to my new friend, as I headed for the stage.

"You're next, Bonnie," I heard him say, coming up behind me.

"You know her? How come I haven't seen her? What does she do?"

"I do. She didn't have to be here. She's a singer."

"And? What else do you know?"

"You haven't got a chance."

"I don't mean personal, I mean, we're competing. Is she good?"

"Like I said . . ."

~~~

Once again, I sat off center on the lip of the stage. My music came up. Though dressed in sweatshirt and jeans, with no make-up, no rocker, I felt comfortable enough while telling the story to glance about the stage. About a third of the way through, I had the staging figured out for tomorrow's full presentation.

For the moment, I felt no nerves, no anxieties. Looking around the room, people stared back, not talking or moving . . . watching. Funny how, at the oddest times, you can feel pieces fall together. Despite the stripped down look, words and emotion clicked, taking the 'Old Man' up a level . . . a level I had not taken it to since arriving in New York.

I noticed a young girl sitting, watching, whispering to Bonnie.

Last word said, last note heard, I was again met with awkward, uneven applause. *'The Hallmark Minute has ended. Do I applaud or change the channel?'*

In the intimacy of Boston coffeehouses, I had come to accept silence as compliment for an artsy-fartsy job well done. Here, in the vast expanse of the Biltmore Ballroom, though feeling more out of my league than ever, I knew from seeing the other adult entries, if I could survive to Sunday night, 'unique' had a shot.

~~~

When Bonnie took the stage, singing the song I would be hearing over and over for the next two days, I didn't know whether to laugh or scream! *'Send in the Clowns!'*

I do believe I shed a tear!

'Oh, you are having a field day up there, aren't you? Aren't you?'

* *. . . my li'l black dad'*. See novel, *'Never Play Leapfrog with a Unicorn'*.

~14~

Cheers, Tears & Autographs

Being alone in New York for almost two days now, going from Main Ballroom to my room, Main Ballroom to my room, Rain Mallboom to . . . was, even though I think I was handling it well, getting on my nerves.

Not wanting to miss Jodi's call . . . *'I did mention the Biltmore . . . I did . . . didn't I? Yes, yes I did. Unless she heard Baltimore. Hot*L Baltimore? No, that's a play. Baltimore . . . Biltmore? They changed it from Biltmore to Baltimore! Playwrights, very clever. I wonder if the Biltmore people know?'* I dared not venture far.

Living off Room Service . . ."Yes, sir. Yes, sir. Yes, sir." *'prick'* was taking its toll on me also.

~~~

9:30 am
Saturday

Acknowledging few, ignoring most, down the hallways, in the elevator, through the lobby, past the Front Desk, *'Don't even look at me!'* I arrived at the Main Ballroom dressed in robe, pajamas, and slippers, sporting a crop of freshly sprayed silver/white hair.

At the center of glares and stares, I helped the bellman unload the side table and rocker from the luggage gurney. Going through the motions of patting myself down, *'A miracle right now would be, well, a miracle.'* hoping against hope I'd find a waylaid tip dollar or two, *'I can't begin to tell you how I appreciate all your help so far.'* I found nothing more than a squished, linty, Junior Mint. *'I bet you flattened that too, didn't you?'*

I was about to pass the hat among the oglers when, "Hell you s'posed to be?" a minor miracle was granted. "Father Time?" Commando Techie grinned.

"Can I ask a favor? Would you tip the bellman? I'll pay you back tonight."

Taking a wad of bills from his pocket, he peeled off a one and . . . that was it. *'Minor and cheap!'* The bellman nodded to Commando Techie, "Thank you, sir." took the bill, "Have a good day." and glanced at it. "Will there be anything else?" *'I know what you're thinking!'* He then looked at me. *'Don't say it!'* "Best of luck to you, sir." *'C'mon, let's have it!'* Grasping the gurney, he walked away.

"You don't know how close you just came."

"To what?"

"Being called a pr—"

'queeeeech' " . . . ick of the trade," said the dapper looking gentleman, standing at the stage mic. "As I was saying, one trick of the trade is keeping a step ahead of your audience . . . do not let them know

what's coming. So, from here on, everything backstage; make-up, wardrobe, anything to do with the show, including entries, that's all of you . . . what belongs backstage *stays* backstage."

"Who's he?" I quizzed Commando Techie.

"Phillip Nolan. He's your man."

"Oh, *he's* the man." I nodded, wiser in knowing.

"No, he's *your* man."

"He's *my* man?"

"Yeah, that's him."

"Oh, *that's* him." I hadn't a clue! Commando Techie walked away, having told me nothing. "Who's he?" I asked the piano playing comic walking by.

"Don't scare me like . . . hey, you're the old guy. I mean old story guy. I get it now . . . robe, chair, white hair. We were worried. Him? That's Phillip Nolan. Executive Director, New York Academy of Theatre Arts. He's the reason we're here."

"He's the man then?"

"Well, I'd be a little more respectful . . ." *'Some days I can't fookin' win!'* "but, yes he is. From what you've been doing in rehearsals, Mr. Nolan's definitely your main focus."

"We?"

"What?"

"You said 'we' were worried."

"Oh," he said, looking away. "The others in the Adult part."

"The 'others'?"

"Well, not all . . . some."

"Some . . . what?"

"We, well, some of the others in the group—"

"Group?"

"Category—"

"Yes?"

"Are you like this all the time?"

"Are they worried?" *'Good! They should be . . . they should all be worried! At least he's man enough to admit it.'* "What's the 'group' worried about?"

He gave me a quick glance then looked away. "Nothing." I caught the smarmy smirk.

"They all think I'm nothing to worry about? Is that what—"

"How'd you like my act?" he asked, ignoring my question.

"When are they moving the piano off the floor up to the stage?"

"I—"

"Couldn't see you past the first three rows."

"Well—"

"What's the point if we can't see you?"

"I—"

"I'd speak to somebody, that's just not right."

"My material's good."

"Be seen, be heard, be understood. Ever heard it? I'd be concerned if I was you." He walked away, his confident smirk replaced by his perplexed brow. *'Fook you!'* I may not have a firm handle on what I'm doing, but I do know why I'm here!

~~~

7:35 pm

The morning trials had not gone as smooth as planned, but it was a showcase compared to the afternoon attempt. I lie in my room knowing I'd be heading home. *'Why don't you just send in the clowns and take me now?'*

'ring'

"Hello. Jodi? It's alright . . . it's alright. I knew you would. It's going okay, I guess. I'll know within the hour. No, no make-up, everything else though. Yeah, did the hair. It's okay. I was noticed. What? That's why you got involved . . . to do the make-up, remember? I've no idea. Never touch the stuff. Today? I did for it for the story. Are you . . . you are? Call about eight-thirty, I'll know then. I'd like to talk about—"

'click'

Jodi didn't.

~~~

8:20 pm

Mostly singers, a couple of dancers, and the piano playing comic, stood huddled, smiling, laughing, back-slapping each other in high spirits of surviving the cut. A mime who had rattled, losing concentration during the evening trials after getting stuck in her imaginary box, breaking her character and apologizing to the Panel, stood off to the side, crying. Her consolation was found in the arms of the ventriloquist, who never quite learned that three minutes of dummy proctology jokes is three minutes too many. The mid-thirties baton twirler, who somehow managed to shoehorn herself into her old high school cheerleading outfit, was the one I felt bad for. Why? I guess I have a soft spot for humiliation.

"Have you seen Bonnie?"

"Did you make it?" asked Commando Techie. "Where's the fookin' list? I never saw it."

"One cut down, one to go." He offered his congratulations. "Thanks. Have you—"

"No, haven't seen her. She's in though."

"I know. I wanted to congratulate her."

"Save it for tomorrow night. You'll see her then."

"Oh." I didn't want to argue. I knew with attendance mandatory for both trials, tomorrow morning and afternoon, I'd see her well before tomorrow night. *Jodi!* "Damn, what time is it?"

"Eight forty-five. That stuff doesn't come out easy, does it?"

"What?"

"The white hair. Why don't you pay someone a few bucks to age you? There's enough fookin' make-up floating around here to—"

"I have someone. Gotta run. See you tomorrow."

I made a beeline from the main room, through the lobby, past the Front Desk, to the oldest, slowest elevator Otis ever installed! Riding up is when it hit me. *I made the cut! I made a New York cut! How cool is that? Fookin' cool is what!* Note to self, *'Make new friend.'*

～～～

5:50 am
Sunday

Out on the sidewalk, I considered my options. *I've never seen the sun rise over the Hudson or crest the New York skyline. Never seen the Empire State or 'Missy Liberty', as my dad called her. 'And, I've never seen the lights go out on Broadway.'* Time enough for one. *'Choose.'*

Standing on the corner of Broadway and 'Yesterday', I watched the nightly neon sputter dim, the sun's rise light 'em back up.

I leisurely wandered, up one side and down the other; that few early morning New Yorkers were out was a multi-blessing. I think it's illegal or, at the very least, grounds for forced institution, to be seen walking about this city sporting such a tattooed grin.

'Broadway deserted on a Sunday morning.' **California Suite.** *'How much of a miracle is this?'* **Death of a Salesman.** *'Alright, okay, you snuck one up on me.'* **Texas Trilogy.** *'It is the little things, isn't it?'* **Pal Joey.** *'Thanks.'* **For Colored Girls Who Have Considered Suicide When the Rainbow is Enuf.** *'Excuse me?'*

~~~

9:05 am

"Morning, sir. Yes, beautiful day for a walk. I have a message for you. There you are. I do, sir. It is exactly six minutes past the hour. Hm? Nine, sir. Time does fly. Nine. Yes, sir. See, the big hand is on . . . You're welcome, sir. You have a good day, sir.' *'If he calls me 'sir' once more . . .* 'Then again, it is better than 'the' look! It is the lesser of . . . *'prick' . . .* two evils.'

In the elevator, I read, *'Spoke to promoter early this AM. Well done! Sorry about last night. Will explain when I see you. Will call for Finals cut to meet you. Unique is good! Miss your face, your smile. Jodi.'*

I knew, I just knew there had to be a good, possibly humorous, explanation for the, at worst, confusion on my part. Though I may have been a bit of a broken record over the past weeks, my New York tunnel vision aside, I knew Jodi knew what needed to be known. There was no doubt in my mind. When we were together life's fog lifted; we fulfilled needs our wants never imagined. At a glance, we shared thoughts, laughing aloud. Just a wisp of breath brought passionate heights; delight brought us to frolicking ends.

'If nothing is perfect, then everything's wrong.' Right? *'Then everything's perfect if nothing is right.'* No doubt, there was something wrong, but not like I was imagining.

What bothered me now, right now? Prior to mentioning it to him, having not been told or having seen the list, how did Commando Techie know Bonnie had made the cut? Had he 'assumed' so? She was pleasant to look at; her voice was okay, but no better or worse than the others.

~~~

Walking through the lobby, heading for the morning competition, it was impossible to miss the large, glitzy sandwich board; a second board, along with a life-size, freestanding, cardboard cut-out, appeared in the Main Ballroom entrance. Seems someone I'd never heard of would be the featured headliner, pro-level entertainment for tonight's Finals.

Commando Techie was right. I'd not seen Bonnie at either trial.

As I sat, waiting for the cuts to be posted, the final thirty known, I couldn't help but stare at the life-size cut-out. Male, early twenties, costumed and posed, holding a mic in typical tacky Las Vegas style; white jumpsuit, white boots, full cape, and a loud, tasteless belt buckle, big enough to double as a marquee. *'Hey, no matter how bad my need to quench this, this 'whatever', pull the plug if it ever gets to that. Okay? Hey? Hey? Hello!'*

I scanned the list of posted thirty finalists. *'I don't care if they dig Ed Sullivan up to host this freak show . . .* 'In appearance order, number twenty-seven . . . *'Are you kidding?'* 'The Old Man' will be on a Manhattan stage! *'What have you done?'*

I made my way from the crowd as cheers, tears, autographs, a lot of hugs, and a few cameras flashed. Glancing for Commando Techie, I spotted him in his glory, dangling from a steel light bar above the crowd. Giving him the thumbs-up, I started to leave. *'That's two in a day. I've heard miracles come in threes. Tonight? I'm taking this, aren't I?'* I had to smile.

"Mister?" I turned to a girl, about eleven years old. It took a second 'til I realized she was the girl I'd seen sitting with Bonnie yesterday. "Can I get your picture?"

"Huh? I, uh, yeah, sure." Hair still white, in pajamas, tattered robe, and slippers, I threw my arm around the tacky, bigger than life, Las Vegas Elvis cut-out.

'click' *'There's a Kodak moment for you.'*

"I saw what you did, five times. I went to see my Grandpa. Will you sign this?"

~~~

'Alright, was she the third one?' I thought, feeling verklempt, *'I'll take it.'* but flushed with laughter as the elevator rose. *'You are a sly one.'* I felt myself grinning. *'You know that, don't you?'*

The doors opened. I sprang from Otis, took a left and, *'bang'!*

'tic'

I walked smack into Jodi.

'flit'

"This is my 'brother'."

'Enough with the miracles already!'

~15~

'Monster with a Thousand Eyes'

There was no introduction to speak of, no words exchanged between Jodi's 'brother' and I, just a glance of supposed understanding.

In very few words, Jodi convinced him she and I would be okay, alone in the room. He followed us down the hall, taking up a magazine, sitting in a small reading area across from my door.

I stood across the room, my back against the wall, looking at Jodi sitting on the bed, make-up bag by her side. I've always had less than no patience for long, drawn out explanations of the obvious so, with a weeks worth of blind assumption, I dove right in. "I'm not going to stand here pretending like I didn't know."

"You knew? No you didn't."

"Yes, I . . ." *It was one thing to suspect, but a slap in the head to hear her admit it; so much for conversational foreplay!* "I had a hunch."

What would normally be considered 'awkward quiet', because of where we were about to go, I would now have to call 'silent sadness'. "So, how long?"

"Six months."

"And I've been with you for two of them. I missed you by a measly four months?"

'flit'

"I know, I know."

'tic'

"I don't know which is worse. That you did this to me at all or that you chose *now* to do *this*. And how did you know to just come along? I only found out myself twenty minutes ago. Or did it matter? Nice day for a ride?"

"I knew if you made it through the first cut . . . unique is good, remember?" She forced a half smile. 'tic' "Are you okay?"

"Am I okay? No, I'm not okay! Why did you bring him? What the hell were you thinking?"

"He offered to drive. He understands. He's really a sweetie."

"Well, gee, thanks for sharing that with me! So what's 'Sweetie' going to do? Sit there 'til the yelling, 'til the name calling starts?"

"Would you rather he come in?"

"I'd rather he drop dead, is what I rather! Who are you? You want to know why I don't believe this? Because . . . because I don't! I can't! I not only have a plainclothes cop outside my door, but he's your husband to boot!"

"He's . . . That's not . . . I'm not married . . ." Jodi stammered, looking at me incredulously.

"You're not? But you—"

"I know you thought it was some code or something, but he really is my brother, and he really is a policeman. It's not all that unusual, you know. I don't know why you can't grasp that."

"So, you're not—"

"No."

'flit' "Well, I couldn't feel anymore fool—"

"Not . . . Yes."

"You are?"

"Yes."

"Then who the hell are you marr . . . Oh no! No! Not . . . Oh, Jodi!"

"Warren's a really nice guy. He's a . . ."

"Shut-up! Just shut-up! Don't you dare call him a sweetie! I've got your sweetie . . . right here! Where's the camera?"

"Camera?"

"C'mon, where'd you hide it? Things like this just do not happen! It's a joke, right? One of those Candid Camera, 'Oops, look at me with my ass hanging out for all the world to see,' things?" Jodi did nothing more than look at me with a smile meant to break my fall. "Don't laugh! Do not fucking laugh! At your doing, do you realize, your husband drove his wife's lover home after their first date! Are you friggin' demented? How? How could you do that to him? To me?"

"Warren didn't mind. He wanted to meet you."

"One of us is sick here and it's not me!"

"It's Warren."

"No, I think it's closer, a lot closer than that! How could you? Why did you even mention my name to him?"

"Warren knew about the first show because I told him. It was no big deal. I was just doing make-up for some guy at a Chinese restaurant. I wouldn't exactly call that a major 'red flag' setting. Then New York came up. I told him, I had to tell him. I couldn't just disappear for four days. Then he found out about the night on Treasure Island."

"Boulder Isle. What'd you do? Run home and tell him all about the stray you found on the beach?"

"No! He was asleep on the couch. I went to bed. Later he woke-up and came upstairs. I was half asleep, I must've been dreaming. When I felt the motion of the bed, of him next to me, I rolled over and said your name. Not once or twice, I don't know how many times or just what I said, but he woke me up asking all kinds of questions."

"But nothing happened. All we did was talk."

"I know. And he believed me. I came to you the next morning to tell you, to say the things I should have said, to tell you the truth, to wish you good luck, but I couldn't." Her chin crinkled, her stiff upper lip softened. "You didn't have to pay attention to me! You didn't have to make me laugh! You didn't . . . or write . . . say things . . . or touch me . . . kiss me like that!"

"You never said not to!"

"Because I wanted you to! I didn't want you to stop! Every time you touched me I had to catch my breath. I thought I had asthma! I've never felt anything like that. With Warren . . . I listen, I look, I smile, I cook. Feelings? I never had to have feelings. Going through the motions has always been good enough! Warren walked me to the school bus, sat with me on the school bus. Asked me to the prom, I said no, he bought the tickets, we went to the prom. He bought the garage, I started teaching. He bought a house, I put up curtains. He bought a bed, and—"

"And you've been getting screwed ever since. Sorry."

"My life has always been so predictable, so boring. I'm twenty-six and I feel so god-damned old! I am so sorry. This is all my fault, you didn't know what you were doing!"

"What I was doing? I knew exactly what I was doing! What did I do that was so wrong?"

"Nothing! Everything! Warren has never made me laugh as hard . . . I don't think he's ever made me laugh at all. I know he's never held me or made love to me as long or as often, certainly never on a pile of rocks, and definitely never ever like *that*! We have sex on Tuesdays, right after Mork and Mindy. It would never occur to him a quickie during the commercials was even possible. I'm numb. I've been numb all my life! You made me feel special, needed. You listened like I had something to say! I didn't fall in love with you because I wanted to . . . I had no choice. I wish I'd never met you! Why did you have to do this to me?"

"And I had a choice? I didn't *have* to . . . I *had* to! I need you . . . I want you now! Right now! If you can't see the obvious . . . Do you love me?"

"Yes."

"Then leave him."

"I did."

"You did?"

"I did!

"Then . . . You did?"

"I did!"

"When?"

"The weekend! This past weekend!"

"What the . . . You might have said something!"

"When he realized I wouldn't be coming home; the neighbors heard a motor running in the garage, knew he never worked Sundays, and found him. That was when my brother called me. That's why I left."

"How is he?"

"He's home. He'll be okay. Warren has always been there for me, I don't know why. I don't know a time he wasn't there; I don't know when he turned into my only friend. I don't even know when I said, when I *actually said*, I'd marry him. One morning I woke-up married to a pair of cold feet and cried for three days!"

"You don't love him."

"I almost killed my best friend."

"You don't love him."

"He has given me so much."

"You do not love him!"

"No! No! I do not love him! It has nothing to do with love!"

"Then why? Why stay with someone who doesn't love you?"

"I never said he didn't love me . . . he does! It's me! Me! I've been Miss Goody Two Shoes for so long, I could scream! I know it's a terrible thing to say, but if I could just replace him with you in the house, at the table, in my bed, in my life—"

"You can . . . right now!"

"No! I can't!"

"Why?"

"I need the white picket fence. I want the babies. You'll never need or love me as much as . . . I'll never be as important to you as the reason you're here tonight! You scare me! Warren goes off to work every morning needing to please no one but himself, not questioning, not confused about what he's all about. All he needs at the end of the day is a warm house, warm meal, and a warm smile. Everyday, you leave a respectable, good paying job, hoping on a dream you'll never have to go back. You put yourself through all these trials, in the name of 'creativity' when nobody's watching, nobody's listening, nobody cares!"

"Get out."

"Fr—"

"I trusted you from the start! I never lied to you . . . you said you understood and you loved it! I'm willing to bet you were in this just for you! You knew from the get-go this wouldn't work, but you kept coming back and coming back. Were you sufficiently entertained? You staged this whole affair thinking about no one but yourself! I know for a fact if we'd met, if all this happened a few months, weeks earlier . . . Did it ever occur to you, but for the sake of weeks . . . years will be lost?"

"Is your phone ringing? Are publishers beating your door down?"

"The only one who's doing any 'beating down' here is you! For once, even if *just once*, something I created made it to a New York stage! Your decision has less than zero to do with what you know is right . . . it's all about money and you know it! Something good just might happen tonight. Do you know what I'm creating tomorrow?"

"No."

"Neither do I, but I'm looking forward to it!" There was a pause, an exchange of fragile, faint smiles . . . an encouraging second I could not leave alone. "You know the difference between you and Shirley?"

"Don't."

"Nothing! How about one last hard one for old time's sake? Here, I'll give you an easy twenty."

"That's not what I came here for."

"Why don't you go? Gather up your stuff, call your bodyguard and leave."

"It's getting late."

"Get out!"

"We should get started."

"You don't think you're going to make me up now, do you?"

"In the beginning, this is what you wanted. Everything else happened while we waited. Please?"

~ ~ ~

Jodi dismissed her brother from his post, telling him to meet her at the Main Ballroom entrance at seven. The backstage call I had was for seven also, with an eight o'clock curtain. At least she'd stay for the show.

I set the desk chair center of the room and sat, head back, eyes closed. The subtle shake of her hand, scent of her near, was impossible to ignore. Dry cotton bits were quick to moisten, as Jodi dabbed make-up around my temples, my eyes. She never said a word as I made what would be my final attempt at putting fate right. "We could, you know.

'tic'

If you came here telling me all you have, but I was the one you chose, I'd walk out of here right now." This told the story of what really should have been. "He won't ever . . . this friggin' hurts! I've never been in love like this." But it wasn't to be. "And they lived happily ever . . . I want a happy ending!"

'tic'

And, as if the little Dutch boy said, "Fuck it!" pulled his finger from the dike and went home, emotions burst, flooding out. Knees buckled, arms flew. "I can make you happy!" One tear drenched kiss after another slipped free of their mark. "There is nothing I . . . to make you mine."

'tic'

Slowly, we gathered ourselves together, accepting the inevitable. "When you leave here, when you're with him, you can smile all you want, but you'll never be happy."

'tic'

"Done," Jodi said. I opened my eyes, looking straight into hers. Teary-eyed puddles piddled down her cheeks.

"How do I look?"

"Tell me a joke," she said, through a quivering smile.

"If the time comes that I look like this for real . . . if it takes that long for you to be free . . . find me."

"That's not a joke."

"No, it's not."

'flit'

'tic'

~~~

We made a very odd-looking couple walking down the halls, down the crowded elevator, through the lobby. "Is that him?" Jodi asked.

I smiled through the pancake. "What you've put this sweet old man through!" The crowd at the Front Desk hushed. "You should be ashamed!" They barely noticed when we burst, laughing, running like fools to the Main Ballroom, intent as they were to deal with the clerk.

"This is . . ." I started to say, introducing Commando Techie to Jodi. "I'm sorry. I don't know your name."

"Les."

"Les, this is Jodi. My . . . make-up person."

"I can see why you waited."

"She did good, eh?"

"Yeah, that too!" *'Down boy . . . she's taken.'*

"Are you placing his set?" asked Jodi, in an officious, yet lighthearted, tone.

"Yes?" he answered, quizzically humored in his defense.

"In relation to the rocker, in stage lingo, where does the side table set?"

"Down center, angled, stage right," Commando Techie reported, and smiled.

"I'm impressed!" Jodi returned the smile, squeezed my hand. I pointed up to two seats I'd taped off, reserved for them. She turned, and with her brother in tow, I watched as they made their way to the balcony entrance.

"She's a keeper. You'd better get backstage."

~~~

Center Stage ~ Biltmore Ballroom ~ Central Park & Broadway ~ New York

'The Roar of the Greasepaint, the Smell of the Crowd,' I thought, grinning, as behind the closed curtain I made my way across the darkened stage. I counted the paces, eleven, and sat down on the pre-set old wicker rocker, stage front center. *'Well, so far, so good. I didn't trip.'*

Though mere seconds ticked by until my 'act' was announced, my name introduced, I felt I had aged a decade. *'How? How in the name of hell did I get here? Oh, now is a fine time to question a moment!'* No time to dally, to ponder. *'Breathe! Concentrate!'*

The heavy, red velvet curtain slowly rose. A spotlight, and a bank of powder blue baby-spots came up, illuminating, framing the staged scene. In front of me, left and right of the center aisle, front to back, rolled a sea of eyes.

'flit'

I looked up to the gilt-edged balcony.

'flit'

But for two empty seats, a wave of eyes stared back.

'flit'

The monster with a thousand eyes waited to be fed.

**To listen 'live', insert 'The Old Man' CD at the start of next chapter. If no CD, go to www.AuthorsDen.com/adstorage/80080/OldMan. mp3

~16~

'Curtain Down'

(insert CD)

For a millisecond *'Jodi'* (blank) I forgot the first word (choke).

Then, as if in disembodied verbal cruise control, the first line of story, my words, committed to a cause, poured forth . . . cloaked in a smooth, put-on, aged tumble.

" . . . . another year past,

'This is it, boy. Stick it! It all comes down to this. You made these three minutes happen. Reach in, grab hold, rip their friggen hearts out!'

ah, but what a year it was.

'Listen. Do you hear it? Do you hear, twerp? Nothing. You got 'em, you got 'em right where you want 'em.'

Now I look across the tables,

'They have no idea what's coming, but you do, bunghole, you do. You wrote it, they're listening.'

see the same old faces,

'Listen. Silence. They were not expecting you. They certainly were not expecting this.'

hear the same old fables.

'They're all yours, boy. What was is no longer. Say hello to what is, knucklehead.'

Oh, for someone to lend me an ear,
I can no more go home for I am here . . .
Deserted by love.

Night stalking nurses, ah, they gotta lend me a hand.

'What's new, what's new in my Promised Land?'

Got no control over what's happenin' now,
sign me away they did.
Now my home is . . .
Oh, but I can see, 'n think, 'n hear a little, too.

Ah, but one thing, one thing Lordy is . . .
I . . . uh, I don't like it Lordy.
No, take me outta here Jesus, this is no life for me.
Ah, but tomorrow for me could be just alright.

Oh, but I remember good days. Drink?
Oh, drink 'til I was half crazed. Even gamble?

Yeah, I gambled my last cent away I did . . .
yeah, yeah, I did.

Ah, they're gonna give up on me, Lordy.
Yeah, they uh, they done left me here to die, but,

oh, no, no, not even, not even gonna cry.
Except, except maybe to you,
whoever, wherever you are. Oh,
ya gotta see your way. Oh,
ya gotta take me outta here! Oh,
ya just gotta take me outta here . . .

Oh, yeah, yeah, I'm an old man lost,
eighty-five years of livin' an this, this is the cost.
Oh, take me, take me outta here Jesus,
ah, this is no life for me, no, no.

But one thing Lordy is, if ya take me,
take me easy, treat me gentle, kind.
'Cause ya see someone, someone did love me . . .
Oh, they did love me."

~~~

I've heard it said, 'Stone-dead silence can be as good as a standing-O.'
My one hope . . . I wasn't the one I heard it from.

Bonnie followed me at number twenty-eight. Jodi certainly
would have laughed at the irony of 'Send in the Clowns' had she
stayed.

Last act presented, the curtain fell. Judges huddled, the crowd
muttered, murmured and mumbled. I stood in the wings, peering
across the darkened stage, watching shadow figures move at a frantic
pace. Totally unexpected, the heavy red velvet flew up, revealing the
night's 'Featured Performer'.

The musical intro, loud and ever building, hit crescendo peak, when
the spotlight burst bright on Las Vegas Elvis. He stood, self-hidden,
behind the raised American Eagle sequined cape. *'Like it or not, that
takes a lot of confidence.'*

The cape fell away to collective whispered gasps. *'A lot of nerve!'*

It was 'Pretty Boy Floyd' imitating, replicating, giving his all duplicating his 'cut-out' look of years gone by. *'And a lot of balls!'* 'See the old lady with the heavy make-up, wearing the fur? She's the bank,' I remember Commando Techie telling me. *'At times I feel sorry for the rich.'*

Ten were called up, then whittled to five. Three were applauded, leaving two. Bonnie and I stood side-by-side, mismatched bookends to be sure. Scoring cards flipped and flashed as the Judges conferred.

"And the winner of . . ."

'Send in the Clowns'.

'How I detest that tune.'

~~~

Now, by nature, I'm not a sore loser. I do rise to competition; try to learn through a loss. But there are times you know, you just know, the winds of change blew smoke right up your arse!

I left the stage, hoping against hope, for one more miracle, *'Let me disappear!'*

Was it really worth all the trouble? Depends. Can equal judgment be made when pitting an assembly-line of well dressed, cover-copy singers, who entertained but one sense, the ear; compared to a white-haired, pajama clad, slipper shod, tattered-robe wearing, rocking chair octogenarian, spewing forth a life that engaged both ear and eye?

Through throngs of people staring, glaring, pointing and gawking, heads shaking in disapproval, like a bull in a faceless china shop, I made my way out. In a blur, I was in my room, pulling, ripping, scrubbing, ridding myself of disillusion.

(ring)

"Mr. Nolan would like to see you in the Main Ballroom."

~~~

"Are you okay?" asked the dapper Mr. Nolan.

"Were you and the other Judges aware I not only staged and presented, but wrote what you saw and heard?"

"I wondered. I had the notion it might have been a scene from a play." *That does not answer my question!* "I'm thinking," *Or does it?* "you would benefit considerably by joining us next month." *They think I 'borrowed' it!* "All expenses paid, of course." *How? Why?* Handing me his card, "Would this fit your plans?"

"I'd rather write for no one than regard a panel of alleged someones!"

"What?"

"It's everywhere, isn't it?" Nothing short of a miracle was going to snap me out of this.

"Are you okay?"

Stepping between us, "I cannot begin to tell you how thrilled I am at the scholarship, Mr. Nolan," Bonnie bubbled brightly. *Will someone please find me a Hari Krishna!* Commando Techie ushered me away.

"What's up?"

"What's up? I just took it up the poop chute! That's what's up!"

"What're you so pissed at? The man offered you a scholarship!"

"Yeah? And how many others did he make the offer to? It means nothing! He has a quota like everyone else. Wouldn't look good, a school with empty seats now, would it? Here, want his card? Mind your manners, you'll get one too!"

"You're lucky I don't put your fookin' lights out!"

"Techie joke?"

"Fook you!"

"No! Fuck you!"

"Leslie!" *'Les? Commando Leslie?'* "Come on, the three of us, let's take a walk." Out in the cool night air, Bonnie told her story. "This is my second time here."

"I know. I thought rehearsals were mandatory?"

"She's not talking rehearsals."

"This is my second year here."

"Good for you. You made it twice."

"No, I was invited this time. Last year, Michael—"

"Pretty Boy Floyd. Las Vegas Elvis," offered Commando Leslie.

"Ah."

"Michael cornered me and asked . . ." Bonnie searched for the right words. "He asked me how much—"

"He asked her how bad she wanted to win." *'How much she wanted?'* "How far would she go—"

"I get it! I get it!"

"My father's a lawyer. When I told him, he called the organizers. He made no bones about shutting them down; threatened lawsuits they would never recover from. I was invited back with a guarantee. All I had to do was show up when I did, don't say a word, put on three good minutes, and they would put right the 'misunderstanding'."

I could do little more than shake my head. "You're a singer. Do you really want a theatre scholarship?"

"Well, it couldn't hurt, but no. It's just a ticket here."

"It never ends, does it?"

"If I were you I'd take Nolan's offer and forget this," Commando Techie advised.

"Of all the songs you had to choose from." I had to chuckle at my self-made horror. "Do you get the ugly trophy too?"

"Yes."

"I wanted that hideous thing as much as the free ride."

"Want a trophy? I'll get you one. Must be a hundred of the fookin' things backstage."

"You did notice," Bonnie began, "at the end, all that was left were singers, me, and you? What do you think would have happened if I weren't here? Do you think I was better than them?"

"Do you think I was better than you?"

Bonnie paused, smiled. "Take his offer. In no time, we'll own this city. You write the shows, Leslie can light them."

"What are you going to do?"

"Be the star, of course."

~~~

Mid-morning Monday

In the early hours, through a full-tilt thundering rain, the Heavens lit in full stage splendor . . . *'Fookin' Leslie! He's doing this! I know it!'* I made my way home.

In a half sleeping stupor, I heard a knock on the door, footsteps cross the kitchen floor, *'Jodi?'* then Rick's voice. "Hey, mailman? What happened? Your car roof . . . it's gone!"

"Yeah, the tear opened up a little."

"A little?" I made my way downstairs. "Hey, Shirley and Raymond eloped Friday."

"Think it'll work?" I asked, walking to the backdoor.

"I doubt it. Saturday he caught her with—"

"Oh, my God!" It was the most bizarre thing I'd ever seen! "I heard the rocker rip through on the Jersey Turnpike, but . . ." The chair had not only ripped through, but somehow settled, intertwined, jutting out of the metal skeletal roof frame. Ravaged flaps of torn, tattered, roof fabric, draped over the body of the car, fluttering in the morning breeze. From the kitchen door, I saw pools of sparkling water in the backseat.

"You drove through like that?"

"I guess it was a little damp. I didn't think it was *that* bad! It was three in the morning." Stunned at the sight, I had to laugh. "Must've had other things on my mind."

"You okay?"

"I've been getting that a lot lately. You in a rush? Why don't you light one up," I suggested. "I've got a story for you."

~~~

Noon

"This his card?" Rick asked, picking a clump of well-soaked pocket trash off the table.

"Yeah." As he went to pass it to me, the card, along with other message scraps from the past few days, dropped to the floor.

"Well, you gave it a shot. Give you credit for that. You still have your job." He handed me the clump with the card, then went back for a last loose scrap of paper. I said nothing. "Right? You didn't quit did you?"

"No."

"The business with Jodi . . . who knows? I can't help you there. As far as the Post Office goes," Rick rose to leave, "you did the right thing. Some dreams are best left at that . . . dreams." He paused, thought, then laughed. "I don't know where the hell that came from, but you'll see." He handed me the scrap and left.

Opening the side window as Rick passed, "Hey, tell Shirley I . . . never mind, forget it. Don't say anything." He grinned, nodded, and went his way.

Looking down the shoreline, for a moment, despite all that had happened over the past two months, I felt like nothing changed. I caught the movement of a couple, hand in hand, laughing, emerging from a Boulder Isle crevice.

In my right hand, I held the business card. 'Phillip Nolan. Executive Director, New York Academy of Theatre Arts' and a phone number. In my left, the scrap. 'Thomas Walker. Postmaster. Call Monday,' followed by a phone number.

'You did the right thing. Some dreams are best left . . . '

~~~

'In the scheme of things, it was a little dream.

In the scheme of dreams, it was everything.'

~~~

"Hello. Mr. Nolan?"